Tom Hanks always stands out as a refreshing presence . . .

Someone we feel we want to know better because he always comes up with the right quip, the funny pun, the off-the-wall comment which loosens everyone up and makes us feel good. When he's on, which is pretty much all the time—especially if the camera is running—Tom Hanks is the idealized view we all have of ourselves as the endlessly witty, ever-inventive, suave, debonair sophisticate who's still capable of emitting a Bronx cheer at a strategic moment.

Tom Hanks, eternal cut-up, ends up becoming the guy who always ends up on top; sometimes—in fact, most of the time—despite his own clumsiness. It is this quality, this basic likability, which has come out in each and every one of Tom Hanks's movies. You wanna know this guy.

TOM HANKS

ROY TRAKIN

A 2M COMMUNICATIONS LTD. PRODUCTION
ST. MARTIN'S PRESS/NEW YORK

Photo research by Amanda Rubin
Cover photo: Globe Photo/Ralph Dominguez

TOM HANKS

Copyright © 1987 by Roy Trakin and 2M Communications Ltd.

Library of Congress Catalog Card Number: 87-60621

ISBN: 0-312-90782-6   Can. ISBN: 0-312-90786-9

Printed in the United States of America

First St. Martin's Press mass market edition/October 1987

10 9 8 7 6 5 4 3 2 1

DEDICATED TO THE ONES I LOVE:

- My wife Jill Merrill
- My parents and my sister

Acknowledgments: Denise Cox, Peter Scolari, Genie Fenton, Judy Shayne, Drew Wheeler, Howard Green, David Chambers, Leonard Ripps, Laura Davis, Craig Modderno, Alana Scott, Jane Kerman, and, of course, my b.w. Jill Merrill, without whom. . . .

INTRODUCTION

Tom Hanks and the "Why Me?" Syndrome

"I've got kind of a bizarre body, a big ass, and fat thighs. I've got a goofy-looking nose, ears that hang down, eyes that look like I'm part-Chinese and are a funny color. I've got really small hands and feet, long limbs, narrow shoulders, and a gut I've got to keep watching. My hair makes me look like a Talmudic scholar." Thus spake one Tom Hanks, describing himself for a recent full-scale *Esquire* magazine fashion spread. Indeed, except for his reported $1 million-a-picture movie salary, thirty-one-year-old Tom Hanks could be you or me, a clever and amiable but definitely vulnerable young urban professional. Why Tom Hanks? You might well ask.

Why Tom Hanks and not Michael Keaton or Tom Cruise or Mickey Rourke or Sean Penn or Andrew McCarthy or Judd Nelson or Jon Cryer or any number of other talented young actors for the star bio treatment? Well, for one thing, knowing today's tabloid, *People*-fed media frenzy, there are probably tomes already in the works on at least five of the above-mentioned new breeders. And my topic happens to be Tom Hanks.

Once again, why? When I tracked down his publicist, at one of the better-known power agencies in Hollywood, even she was a little bewildered.

"Why Tom Hanks?" she queried over the phone when I informed her, hoping for an interview, that I was writing a biography of one of her clients. "What are you going to say about someone who's done only eight movies?"

Her surprisingly sarcastic attitude was audible over the line. While I'd hardly expected her to do cartwheels, fully aware that unauthorized biographies tend to be frowned upon by agents as well as the stars themselves, who obviously prefer the control inherent in "official" self-penned or ghostwritten stories, I was still a bit taken aback by the seemingly small regard she had for the career of one of America's most popular actors.

Yes, it's true. "Most popular" is not hyperbole. Very quietly but very steadily, and through the accumulation of good to great work in the midst of some questionable vehicles, Tom Hanks has staked his ground as one of our leading movie stars. With—this cannot be overstressed—a current asking price of a cool one million smackers per screen appearance. That's a lot of money for a guy who's had but one bona fide box office success to his credit: the $60-million-grossing *Splash*, which was his debut as a leading man. In fact, only two of his other six films—*Bachelor Party* and *Nothing in Common*—were even qualified successes. The rest were out-and-out bombs at the box office and, in most cases, with the critics. These included such films as *Volunteers*, *The Man with One Red Shoe*, *The Money Pit*, and an Israeli film, *Every Time We Say Goodbye*, his only serious role.

So, when colleagues and friends asked me

what I was possibly going to write about in a biography of Tom Hanks, I blithely replied that I'd be doing semiological analyses of *Bachelor Party.* It seemed a hopeless task on any kind of serious, scholarly level. Especially if Tom wouldn't talk to me. And by the way his publicists were protecting him, it was clear that getting face to face with the man himself would be little more than an impossible dream.

But that was not the end of the world, because Tom Hanks has, more often than not, lived out his relatively brief career very much in public. Though an intensely private man about his family, young Hanks has done an admirable job of letting it all hang out for a variety of publications. He's been interviewed and profiled extensively for each of his films, all of them high-visibility, big-studio projects. He's talked at length about his childhood, his college years, his apprenticeship in repertory theater, his days as a starving actor in New York, his marriage, his separation . . . and that tale is here, although it is not at all the whole story.

For a young actor, Tom Hanks boasts an amazing body of work. And a lot of it. Of course, the majority of his filmed experience comes in the thirty-eight episodes of the short-lived television series, *Bosom Buddies*, in which he costarred with Peter Scolari. A major portion of our story will deal with that historic television sitcom and the classic comedy of Hanks and Scolari, which made it so. Their relationship, a very special one, goes a long way toward revealing the depths of Tom Hanks's character.

Even in films that were duds, though, Tom Hanks always stands out as a refreshing presence, someone we feel we want to know better because he always comes up with the right quip, the funny pun, the off-the-wall comment which loosens everyone up and makes us feel good. When he's on, which is pretty much all the time—especially if the camera is running—Tom Hanks is the idealized view we all have of ourselves as the endlessly witty, ever-inventive, suave, debonair sophisticate who's still capable of emitting a Bronx cheer at a strategic moment. Tom Hanks, eternal cut-up, ends up becoming the guy who always ends up on top; sometimes—in fact, most of the time—despite his own clumsiness. It's an attractive self-image, one that's been promulgated by a variety of movie stars Tom Hanks has been compared to, among them Jimmy Stewart,

Cary Grant, Jack Lemmon, Henry Fonda, and Bill Murray.

It is this quality, this basic likability, which has come out in each and every one of Tom Hanks's movies. You wanna know this guy. He's fun to be around. Hanks's effortless amiability comes across quite strongly on the screen.

There's a magic sense about Tom Hanks, almost as if he's living out our own most deeply felt fantasies, whether it's by marrying the mermaid of one's dreams, or by building a house, or by thwarting enemy agents, or by having one last fling before marriage, or by marrying a nice Israeli girl, or by being a top advertising executive. Or even by dressing up as a girl to live in a women's hotel. Hanks has performed all these roles, and notice how many of them deal with wish fulfillment. For nearly every television viewer or movie fan, it's intensely satisfying when someone as ordinary as Tom Hanks, complete with those big lips, fat thighs, and a gut he has to keep on watching, receives his chance to come out on top through the force of sheer will . . . as well as with a quick-on-his-feet ability to pop up with a perfect rejoinder. (Tom Hanks has honed that skill into a fine art.)

For this son of a San Francisco chef, who grew up in a constantly shifting and slightly unusual family atmosphere, is pretty sharp with an ad-lib. Both *Bosom Buddies* and his movies show Hanks to be a master of the drop-dead comeback. In *Splash,* when Daryl Hannah's mermaid breaks every television set in the Bloomingdale's showroom with her telekinetic powers, Hanks deadpans to the stunned clerk, "How about those Knicks?" In *Bachelor Party,* when one of his friends rents a film called *Nymphos without Pants,* Hanks retorts with a straight face, "Olivier's in that, right?" We will leave any number of classic Hanks–Scolari epiphanies until the chapter on *Bosom Buddies,* but at this point it will suffice to say that Tom would more likely than not break into one of his Curly (of the Three Stooges) impressions at a moment's notice.

But what is most interesting to me about Tom Hanks is the simple fact that he seems like a pretty regular guy. And his manager, Si Maslow, who answered his own phone when I dialed his New York number, confirmed that impression. He is confident that Tom is one of the leading actors in Hollywood, but he also knows that reputation isn't built so much on reality as it is on the illusion of success. Take the *Esquire* magazine covers, for example, or the tabloids . . . even those *Bosom Buddies* episodes currently running in syndication. At first Si, who has been Hanks's manager for a number of years, was all too willing to cooperate, even promising to get me to one of Tom's standup appearances around town, one of the actor's methods of preparation for his role as a comic in the upcoming *Punchline*, also starring Sally Field. But a quick phone call to the publicists in charge made it clear that cooperation was not to be.

Which is just as well, because I was able to concentrate on the man's career with a degree of equanimity and objectivity. After all, Tom Hanks represents a throwback to an extremely natural acting style, one in which the method is invisible yet tied, nevertheless, directly to the classical tradition. For unlike many of his so-called peers, actors who graduated from improvisational companies like SCTV, Second City, or *Saturday Night Live*, Hanks's background was in the theater. He immersed himself in the stage early on in his life and literally worked his way through all the dirty work and low-level jobs, from lighting and set design to stitching costumes and selling tickets. Hanks, of course, was trained in the classics after spending a number of years in repertory companies in Cleveland and New York. What seems to have come so easily turns out to have been extremely hard work, which is probably why Tom Hanks is such a private man. He saves his best face for the public, and doesn't want the illusion punctured by the intrusion of harsh reality, tending as it does to reveal personal foibles. And Tom Hanks is nothing if not a very guarded individual.

At the exalted age of thirty-one, Tom Hanks is the perfect age to stand in for that Madison Avenue creation of baby-boomer culture: the Yuppie. More than any other current movie star, Tom Hanks has acted out the dreams and aspirations of the Yuppie on the silver screen. He's run his father's business in *Splash*, he was a rock'n'roll lawyer in *The Money Pit*, a concert violinist in *The Man with One Red Shoe*, a social-climbing young bus driver in *Bachelor Party*, and a pre-Yuppie preppie in the Peace Corps in *Volunteers*.

Like many other Yuppies, Hanks was born just a touch too late to really become a part of the counterculture, yet still close enough to it to be able to relate to a certain something missing from his life in terms of spirituality. That duality—between material happiness and spiritual unrest—returns as a theme in much of Tom Hanks's work, from *Bosom Buddies* through his most realized role, *Nothing in Common*.

Doughboy face and lumpy body aside, Tom Hanks ends up with a beautiful woman in each of his films: Daryl Hannah in *Splash*, Tawny Kitaen in *Bachelor Party*, Lori Singer in *The Man with One Red Shoe*, Rita Wilson in *Volunteers*, Shelley Long in *The Money Pit*, Sela Ward in *Nothing in Common;* as well as Donna Dixon in *Bosom Buddies*. It is, of course, the way he wins over these luscious females that ends up winning over the moviegoer's admiration. Not through sheer aggressive pushiness or macho narcissism, but with never-say-die charm, turning every pratfall to quicksilver advantage and more points for "cuteness." Without doubt, Tom Hanks is the stand-in for every one of us who ever dreamed of getting the girl—while remaining mired in our less-than-perfect bodies, of course—with the perfectly timed witty remark, the hip rejoinder, the *bon mot* to end all *bon mots*. . . . Like Woody Allen as Humphrey Bogart in *Play It Again, Sam.* Or Cary Grant in *Notorious.* Tom Hanks brings back that kind of romance, with the flip attitude of the postmodern hipster.

"I would hope to come off as a guy that's hip," Hanks confessed to *Esquire* magazine. "Richard III was hip. Iago was hip. Brando. *Star Trek.* And of course, Cary Grant. He was the embodiment of hip."

Keeping your cool in a world gone mad. . . .

"We live in very confused times. The rules are constantly being rewritten on us. But it's okay. Civilization is not crumbling at our feet—and those of us who are hip to this and can adjust are going to be just fine."

Which, as *Esquire* doesn't fail to point out, makes Tom Hanks perhaps the perfect actor for our era. All right, admittedly he's not Gerard Depardieu, but then again who is? He may not be a committed, politically motivated performer, but that's not what Hollywood and American movie-making is all about. It's more about dreaming of a possible perfect world, one within reach, than militantly demanding to change this quite faulty one in which we live. And Tom Hanks is a believer . . . in retaining a semblance of grace under pressure, in a willingness to abandon practicality in the pursuit of heartfelt dreams (whether this means joining a beloved mermaid in the ocean or surviving the unmitigated deterioration of a longed-for home). The audience in the 1980s is drawn to Tom Hanks as it once was to similar bumbling dreamers like Jimmy Stewart or Henry Fonda. Except this time, those dreams have emerged from a common core of post-Beatles popular culture and media-drenched trivial pursuits.

If Tom Hanks were nothing more than a spoiled, selfish Brat Packster seeking hedonistic fulfillment, you might as well turn to something more akin to the Judd Nelson story, for example. Through *The Money Pit,* one might be tempted to dismiss Hanks as another glibly precocious movie star who hasn't fully paid his dues. But *Nothing in Common* helped change all that. While its first half showed Tom playing the by-now stereotypical wisecracking yupster, the last portion of the Garry Marshall movie proved, even more than his so-called dramatic role in Moshe Mizrahi's *Every Time We Say Goodbye,* that Hanks was willing to stretch beyond what had proven successful to show a completely different side of himself.

Of course, the film's subplot, with Jackie Gleason and Eva Marie Saint as Hanks's parents, did tend towards the three-Kleenex weepie side, but the theme—that today's Yuppies will soon be responsible for the fates of their parents—was an undeniably powerful one, and one that Tom pulled off with aplomb.

It is because no matter how rich, successful, witty, beloved by our colleagues, and blessed we are, we all go one-to-one with our Maker in the end. Tom Hanks seems to have the ability to plumb the depths of his soul as well as flip off the punchline. For many young American actors, it would be a joke to suggest that they could tackle the classics. Sean Penn as Romeo? Emilio Estevez as Prince Hal? Could you believe Tom Cruise as Hamlet? That thought may be risible for the star of *Top Gun*, yet it would be much less surprising if, one day, Tom Hanks played the role of the melancholy Dane. Or, as he would put it, "Olivier's in that, right?"

Returning to the original question: Why Tom Hanks? Not simply because he's there, but because he's made a difference. He's the kind of actor who's played roles where the characters look skyward and wonder aloud, "Why me?" Why do I have to fall in love with a mermaid? Why do I have to be the host of this bachelor party? How did I get to be the target of rival C.I.A. factions? How did I get aboard this Peace Corps plane bound for Thailand, and all the passengers keep singing "Michael Row Your Boat Ashore"? How could I have bought this lemon of a house that won't stop falling down around me? Why are my parents choosing this time, when I'm at my professional peak, to separate, to get sick, to die? Why did I have to fall in love with this Israeli girl? Why me?

Because the Lord above only tests those He loves the most, and Tom Hanks, a devout Catholic, understands only too well His system of checks and balances. Therefore, when he does get the girl, whether it's beautiful Donna Dixon or nearly naked Daryl Hannah, he can't quite believe his good fortune. And that hesitation, that wink past the imaginary fourth wall to the audience beyond the screen, is what wins us over. How can we not share the life and loves of this character? We all have something in common with him.

1 Growing Up Absurd

"It was a wild, swinging experience. We had a classic kind of split-up family, with remarriages galore and moving around a lot. My dad was in the restaurant business, so, at a moment's notice, we'd be gone, packed up and out of there. It was great. I never got into trouble. I never had problems making friends."

—Tom Hanks

What does hip mean? Its derivation comes from the expression, "from the hip." As in shooting from the hip, as in drawing your gun faster than the next guy, as in being able to think and react by the seat of your pants. In the Old West, those who drew the quickest earned the most respect. Every situation was settled, as one might see in a neurotic Nicholas Ray western, by the draw. In today's civilized, postpunk Yuppie times, the quip has become the gun. He who cracks wise cracks best. It's a defense, and it may well be the best one we have. After all, who makes better use of it than our very own fearless actor/leader, Ronald Reagan? In fact, the art of acting has been raised (lowered?) to the level of the political arena.

Of course, that's not Tom Hanks's fault, but it does go a long way to explaining his success in television and motion pictures. He is quick-witted, but his fast mind merely serves to make up for a very ordinary yet undeniably cute face and body. It is, instead, Tom Hanks's ability to come across as a regular guy that remains at the core of his effectiveness, and such a chameleonlike quality stems straight from his hectic upbringing. As a populist hero, Hanks had a childhood straight out of a Frank Capra movie.

He was born on July 9, 1956 to Amos and Janet Hanks in Concord, California. Tom was the third of four children, with an older brother Larry, sister Sandra, and younger brother Jim. Amos has been described as a restaurateur or chef; whatever he was, he moved around quite a lot, taking along his growing family with him.

The effect of all the tumult on young Tom

cannot be minimized. Perhaps searching for his own kind of stability, he created worlds of his own, as children are wont to do, including stargazing.

"I was really into planetariums when I was a youngster," he told *Us* magazine. "I had a little telescope and, at times, could name all the stars. . . . "

When asked by *Family Weekly* whether he'd imagine things when he was a kid, he said, "Oh yes. I was totally happy being in a room all by myself. When nobody was home, it was the greatest. I could walk around, put on music, sing and dance . . . whatever. I was always very happy just being by myself."

Time alone must have been a precious commodity in the Hanks's household. Tom also tried to compete for the attentions and affections of those around him, always insisting he had a close family despite the domestic turmoil and constant packing up from home to home. Tom later would tell *Rolling Stone* that he was merely the second funniest member of his family. He claimed that his brother Larry, four years older and now an entomologist at the University of Maryland, was always more humorous than he was, typical of Tom's humble quality. His sister runs a news service and Jim, the youngest, is a student living with his mother.

"People used to say, 'Tom's loud,' and then they'd say, 'But Larry—now *Larry's* funny.'"

But his brother, interviewed in 1984 by the *Washington Post,* had a different story: "Tom has always been outgoing, always liked talking to people. And he could always talk to people better than I could."

Indeed, Tom responded to his transient home situation with all the aplomb and ad-lib ability he'd later display on *Bosom Buddies* and in his movies. He adapted. He survived. By shooting from the hip. . . Larry claimed his little brother was the class clown.

"In high school, he [Tom] used to borrow my tape recorder and do kind of his own radio news reports. They were pretty awful. I discovered them only later. You know, like he would announce urgently that an earthquake was coming. 'Leave the city immediately,' that type of thing. I still have the tapes—it's great bribing material that might come in handy someday."

"Everyone in my family likes each other," Tom Hanks told *Rolling Stone,* "but there were always about fifty people at the house. I didn't exactly feel like an outsider, but I was sort of outside of it."

That emotional detachment was to mark Hanks's development as an actor. Always looking from the outside, making the flippant remark rather than facing up to whatever painful reality actually existed. It was a defense mechanism which he would develop into a craft.

Amos and Janet Hanks divorced for the first time when Tom was five. He was later to say that his father wanted to keep having kids because he could afford them, while his mom didn't. They were divorced and remarried "any number of times"—a situation Tom insisted that "we never viewed as being particularly unique."

"We were just a completely more or less normal broken family," he told the New York *Daily News.* "Everybody was married a bunch and everybody lived different places, and nobody thought much of it. It was pretty pragmatic—everybody called their own shots."

He told *Seventeen* nearly the same thing, crediting his early vagabond home life with "making me very flexible. I never thought twice about picking up, changing schools and cities. I came to like it a lot because there were always new things to discover. Even if it was only the different social perspectives of the neighborhoods we lived in, the architecture of the schools I went to—from a portable bungalow to a big classroom with overhead projectors . . . I just felt, 'Hey, this is different!' This school is older than the school was before. The blackboard is different, these desks are different. This is neat. I just hopped around and saw what was happening, like, 'Hey guys, how you doin'?' I was a geeky kid."

Precisely the kind of quick study that marks an actor . . . or a cutup who can quickly deflect the surliest opponent. Yet Tom's more dreamy, introspective interior life must have been difficult to communicate to others, so he assumed a brash but lovable cockiness which made up in one-liners what it lacked in warmth. Hanks has admitted that this has been his problem in establishing close relationships, but he has always refused to blame it on his upbringing.

"More than anything else, the constant flux made me rely on myself for my own entertainment, my own disciplinary values. It also taught me how to travel light—you don't need a whole lot to get by."

When the final split came between Tom's mother and father, he was ten years old. He and his older brother and sister stayed with their father, while his younger brother lived with their mother.

"It's a curious thing," Hanks said in a *Cosmopolitan* interview. "I lived with my dad the longest of any of the kids, but I'm probably the most opposite of him personality-wise." Ironically, he singled out the one trait possessed by his dad which he blames for his own shortcomings in personal relationships, including his divorce. For a guy as quick with a quip, always the life of the party as Tom is, he has intimated that he feels he cannot communicate.

"My dad is essentially a quiet and shy guy," said Tom. "Just recently now, he's been given over to a great ability to communicate, but before that, it was just all balled-up inside all of us. We didn't communicate a lot."

Amos eventually married a Chinese lady named Frances Wong, who had her own family, which sometimes numbered up to twenty-two (and all living at the house). By the time Tom went to junior high, he and his father were settled in Oakland, California, across the bay from San Francisco. Tom liked school, even if he wasn't a particularly brilliant student.

"I never got into trouble," he said, though he did remember himself as "a daydreamer and a jerk." How many would remember themselves otherwise?

"For a while, I spelled my first name Thom but decided spelling my last name Hanx would be dumb," he recalled. "My idea of a good time growing up was taking a bus to Sacramento."

He attended Oakland's Skyline High School. "We had two thousand people there, with an energy I never saw anyplace else. I ate a lot of really bad food, and I ran track and played soccer. I didn't do all that well, but I figured team sports were part of the high school experience."

Even then, Hanks described himself as having "an old head on young shoulders." The competitive nature he had honed in an extremely overcrowded household was just the background he actually drew upon to succeed. "You could get lost in the shuffle or you could be a loudmouth," he once said in a *Mademoiselle* interview. "I chose the latter route. My apprenticeship years, I call them."

It was only a matter of time before the self-proclaimed "loudmouthed goof-off" found his true metier—acting. It was a decision that was neither encouraged nor discouraged by his family.

"We had a pretty *laissez-faire* relationship," he said to the *Los Angeles Times*. "I pretty much called my own shots. I was the third kid and by the time you come along, the folks—well, they pretty much don't care. I mean, it's—'Are you coming home any time soon? Are you in jail?'

"We're all pretty close now, but it was rough for a while. My dad's third wife, Frances, is a wonderful lady, but we made it very hard on her at first. We were awful. There was lots of tension and craziness, for all the classic reasons.

"I was only ten when she came along and I'd been living alone with my dad for a long time and it was like—no one's going to tell me what to do. It took a while to adjust."

It was making people laugh, though, that first gave Hanks a taste of performing.

"I was always the guy in the back of the class cracking people up during the slides," he said. "I realize how that can come out of personal insecurities or as a defensive measure or as a way of craving affection, but I

simply needed an outlet for the expulsion of
energy, which I had but had nowhere to go
with. It was both physical—the idea of working off a sweat—and mental. I wanted to get
involved in the creative process. Not so much
as an actor, but a stage manager or carpenter
or whatever—just to take a part in the energy
that is spent in creating magic."

He has also admitted that one of the most
influential films in his upbringing was Stanley
Kubrick's *2001*, which he saw as a thirteen-
year-old. It changed his life because "it presented to me an entire world of artistic con-
ception that was totally alien to me. I've seen
it twelve times and I don't know why exactly.
I just did. It did everything to me a great
movie should do and I found it extremely
witty." Another early movie which capti-
vated him was Kurosawa's *Seven Samurai*.
"I saw it in junior high school on TV and I
realized I sat there for three-and-a-half hours
reading subtitles. I was completely mesmerized . . . I still suffer from that. I have diffi-
culty just seeing movies for movies' sake. I
want to invest time in it, leave myself open
to it."

That intensely spiritual quality is the other
side to the Tom Hanks coin, and one that is

rarely shown in public. It's no mistake that young Hanks was initially drawn to the technical side of theater, though he did perform in a school production of *South Pacific*. For, in high school, according to his *Bosom Buddies* costar Peter Scolari, Tom was an out-and-out Jesus freak, who proselytized openly and quoted from the Bible. Strangely enough, this theme of martyrdom and earthly sacrifice would resurface in the most unlikely film, the hardly earth-shattering 1981 made-for-TV movie Tom starred in based on the Rona Jaffe novel, *Mazes and Monsters*.

"I was already an actor by the time I decided to become one," he has said. "I never had a dream to become a Hollywood star and drive a gold-plated Cadillac. I really didn't decide I wanted to be an actor until after I had my first acting job."

After graduating high school with a straight-C average, Hanks entered Chabot Junior College in Hayward, California.

"You know how you can send your SAT scores to three schools?" he asked. "I sent one to MIT, one to Villanova, and one to Chabot. I was hoping to get a sticker or something from one of those schools; it'd be nice to have a sticker on the back of the car. But

I went to Chabot, so I cut off the 'Chabot' from the sticker and had just 'College' in back to prove I was a student."

By the time he got to Chabot, the acting bug bit him irrevocably.

"I fell into drama class; something about the life that went along with the theater affected me even then. Being an actor was fun! You'd hang around, get into makeup and wardrobe, and go onstage under those amber gels—that was very romantic." But not enough for a compulsive teenager hungering for total involvement. "Being a stage manager was even more fun than acting. From the moment you walked into the theater, you were busy until you left."

While attending junior college for two years, Hanks also worked at one of the local Hilton hotels as a bellhop, an experience he was certain prepared him for acting.

"It was exactly like acting," he claimed. "You're taking some guy up to his room, you've got to size him up, figure out what he wants to hear, what he wants to find out about. Whether he wants to talk to you at all. Whether he's drunk or not. Same thing dealing with people—you're like an ambassador.

"You put on your bellman suit and then perform the bellman role," he told *Seven-*

teen. "It's the greatest job, carrying bags for sports and entertainment figures. I carried Cher's bags when she was married to Greg Allman. I gave Sidney Poitier a ride to the airport. You make good tips and a nice wage, working three, four days a week, and you're in a position of responsibility because you represent the hotel."

He remembered this period fondly. "I had a job and a girlfriend and a car," he said. "I had everything I needed, bouncing all over the Bay Area. I was in the thick of things, seeing what would happen."

Hanks had discovered the theater in large part due to a Chabot College class called Drama in Performance, which he signed up for because "I was tired of zoology and sociology." It was a course that changed the direction of his life.

"Everyone who signed up thought it was an acting class," said Tom, "but it wasn't. The curriculum included reading plays that were being produced in the Bay Area and then going to see them. The idea was not only to study the plays in their written form, but to see them as well."

With the salary he earned working part-time, Tom often went to shows in nearby San Francisco. With a live theater boom going on in that city during the midseventies, Tom was able to see classics by great playwrights such as Ibsen, Chekhov, and Shakespeare in theaters ranging from 150 to 2,000 seats.

"I thought going to see a play was a great way to spend an evening, but I couldn't convince any of my friends to join me. Before, I had essentially been a child of television. Now, instead of going to basketball games or skiing on weekends, I was bombarded with all these ideas. I was just swept away, really shaken . . . impressed by how actors could get up on the stage and communicate from a blueprint a guy had made forty years before! Here it was, coming to life—you could almost reach out and touch it. I didn't so much decide to become an actor as I decided that working in the theater connected me to an amazing source of energy I wasn't going to find anywhere else. I wanted to be part of it!"

One of the assigned scripts was Eugene O'Neill's intense drama, *The Iceman Cometh*, which was playing at the Berkeley Repertory Theater. At that time it starred Bob Hirschfeld and Joe Spano, who both became featured players on *Hill Street Blues.*

"When I arrived there, I didn't know what to expect. The playhouse was this old run-down storefront. There was barely a stage and the lights looked as if they were going to fall on our heads any moment. As it turned out, I ended up completely mesmerized for the entire four-and-a-half-hour performance. It was the turning point of my life. The awesome power of the play, the performances, everything and everyone was so intense—something inside of me just clicked. By the end of the night, I had a goal in life.

"I developed an instant respect for everyone involved, not just the actors, but the director, stage crew, lighting people, set designers—everyone who could work together to bring an audience a new sense of awareness. That's what really got to me.

"Even though I call this my turning point, and I did end up an actor, I have to stress that because of that performance I didn't decide to become an actor. It was so much more than that. I didn't care what I did—build sets, string lights, paint props, or act—the main thing was to somehow be a part of this life. I knew it would make me happy."

The youngster who'd lived through a constant roadshow as a child found, on the stage, an extended family like the one he'd left behind.

"Because of the impact of that particular

play, it instilled in me a sense of what it was like to be a part of something where everyone was giving their best. And it set a precedent for almost everything I've done since. It taught me to strive to be the best in any situation, by showing me that the best could exist even under the most adverse conditions. It also taught me not to be afraid to set high goals. Even if you never reach those goals, just knowing that you gave it everything you had each step of the way is success itself."

The stage life of Tom Hanks had begun. . . .

2 Go East Young Man

"I was about twenty, basically doing what your average kid does, working, going to college part-time," mused Tom Hanks. "I had three hundred dollars in the bank and gas in my Volkswagen."

Reading and seeing *The Iceman Cometh* galvanized young Tom. He earned a scholarship to California State University in Sacramento in 1976, where he began seriously considering an acting career.

"I went there because they had a very small, very accessible theater arts department in which all you had to do was have the desire to take part in whatever aspect of theater production you wanted to do. Mostly I wanted to learn the technical aspect. I wanted to learn how to build sets. My scholarship was as a stage carpenter.

"Whatever you wanted to do, you did. Want to run the lights? Bang, zoom, there you are at the dimmer board. Work in the shop? Okay, build this, this, this, and this. Twenty-four hours a day, you were surrounded by other interested people, everybody striving for some kind of excellence."

It was at Cal State in Sacramento, in a hotel room full of actors, that Tom met an aspiring producer/actress by the name of Susan Dillingham. Just like many a character he's played in the movies, Tom eventually melted the fellow student's initial cold shoulder and the two became inseparable. Soon afterward, for whatever "professional" reasons, Susan Dillingham changed her name to Samantha Lewes. The relationship continued, fueled by the pair's theatrical desires and ambitions.

Hanks took part in a production of Chekhov's *The Cherry Orchard* at the Sacramento Civic Theater during his first year as a Cal State student. The play was directed by Vincent Dowling, the artistic director of the Great Lakes Shakespeare Festival in Cleveland, Ohio. After the play was over, Dowling, who would turn out to be an important fatherly influence in Hanks's life, invited a number of the cast members to return with him to work the summer season as nonpaid interns. He said the experience would be good because there'd be small roles for them.

"I had nothing better to do and I had never been outside California, so the five of us [including Samantha *née* Susan] threw everything into the back of various cars and drove to Cleveland at the end of the school year." He never made it back to school, to graduate. One summer stretched out into three seasons. Tom immersed himself in all aspects of the theater at Great Lakes—hanging lights, painting sets—until, finally, he realized he wanted to be onstage and not behind the scenery.

"To be honest, the first taste of success I had was when I was working at the Shakespeare Festival and just getting paid for what I was doing. This was a phenomenon to me. This was huge in my eyes."

In three seasons with Great Lakes, Hanks played a variety of roles, starting with the part of Grumio in Shakespeare's *The Taming of the Shrew*. In addition to these thespian activities, though, Tom Hanks developed an underdog's fondness for that town's baseball team, the woeful Cleveland Indians. During off-days at the theater, Hanks would often find himself at 80,000-seat Cleveland Municipal Stadium, on the shores of Lake Erie, tracking the team's seemingly annual descent to the bottom of the American League East. After all, this is a ball club that hasn't won anything since 1954, when it captured the American League Pennant with 111 victories and a pitching staff headed by future Hall of Famers Early Wynn and Bob Lemon, only to be defeated in the World Series by the New York Giants on a great over-the-shoulder grab of a Vic Wertz line drive by Willie Mays and a record pinch-hitting performance by one Dusty Rhodes. To understand Tom Hanks, the average man, you must understand his obsession with the lowly Cleveland Indians. As *Rolling Stone* put it in its profile of the actor, you almost have the feeling that he's "perfectly happy with their position at the bottom of the standings."

"I loved Cleveland," he has said. "After all, I lived there for the last year of my official youth. I really got my stripes as a repertory actor, which means I did a lot of shitty roles. And I spent a lot of days at the ballpark, in that huge stadium with maybe three thousand people. It was sort of an intimate experience."

As an intern at the Festival, he also received a three-year crash course in everything from lighting to set design to stage managing. In between, he flew back to Sacramento, where he served as associate technical director and furthered his education in learning how to "build shows." But the acting bug stayed with him. He went on to play Rosencrantz in *Hamlet*, Montano in *Othello*, Fabian in *Twelfth Night*, and Faulconbridge in *King John*. The apprentice who was originally brought to Cleveland as a spear carrier had begun to master his craft.

In 1978, Tom Hanks received his first public recognition, a Best Actor nod from the Cleveland Critic's Circle for his sixty-eight performances as the caddish Proteus in *The Two Gentlemen of Verona*, which as *New York* magazine pointed out, "also happened to be the last time Hanks ever played anything remotely resembling a bad guy."

"Suddenly, I had *beaucoup* responsibility.

I couldn't go out and smoke and drink, even at twenty, 'cause I couldn't rip my throat to shreds. You're like a mountain climber out there on that stage, and you let something slip, you can die a horrible death. Except the next night, you get to attempt to do it all over again.

"I was only twenty, but I had lucked into the type of training almost impossible for an American actor to get nowadays."

During those three extended "summers," which lasted from May to mid-November, Hanks was able to take on six parts a season in everything from Shakespeare to O'Casey.

"That's one reason why when one job is over, I'm ready to take on the next."

By this time, Tom was ready to make the move to New York and all its theatrical opportunities, and he brought Samantha with him, or had to, seeing as she was just about to give birth. Raised a devout Catholic, Hanks wouldn't hear of an abortion, so the two were married and set out to make it as actors in the Big Apple. They took an apartment on W. 45th Street and he made the rounds of agents, which must have been difficult for Samantha. Tom joined the Riverside Shakespeare Company as an unpaid classical actor, appearing as Callimaco in *The Mandrake* and Hortensio in *The Taming of the Shrew.* But, with a newborn son, Colin, and a wife to support, Hanks was in dire straights.

"Even though working in a Shakespearean repertory company is the greatest training in the world, if it's all you've done, people begin to look at you askance. They start thinking you've got a dog named Horatio or a parrot named Rosencrantz. The truth is, if the acting hadn't worked out, I was willing to do anything. I love the acting, but it's the experience of theater as a whole that I fell in love with most.

"It was important to have that time to do nothing but pursue the work, like a twenty-four-hour-a-day job; either looking for work, trying to improve yours, or examining other people's. Then sitting around drinking coffee with friends and talking about high ideas.

"It was terrible. It was fabulous. It took us awhile to get our bearings and to start making some headway," he reminisced for *Drama-Logue* magazine. "I was lucky because the Great Lakes Shakespeare Festival gave me a full year's income and then a half-year of unemployment compensation. New York is like Los Angeles in the sense you have to fight to get a nonpaying showcase. It seems to me your fate is much more in your own hands in New York than it is in Los Angeles. It relies much less on outside influence in New York."

Despite it all, the struggling Hanks family managed to pull through.

"I got twenty-five dollars once for doing a play in the City Court Building—after rehearsing for four weekends. I was appearing in a production of *The Mandrake* and one of the girls in the show knew a manager who was looking for somebody. I went up and had a marathon meeting with him. He said, 'I'm going to send you out and get some feedback,' which he did. I met a variety of agents. He called me up the next day and we solidified our business relationship."

That deal gave Tom the ability to go back for his last season at Great Lakes in the summer of 1979. When he returned to New York that fall, there was a job, a part in a slice-and-dice film called *He Knows You're Alone*, which now takes its place alongside greats like *The Silver Chalice* (Paul Newman) and *The Blob* (Steve McQueen) as introducing star talent to the screen.

Hanks plays Elliot, a psychology student,

in a very bit part. "I just played a guy," he said. "I wasn't in anything spectacular. I just come in and say, 'How do you do?' and leave. I don't even get killed as I remember. They made the movie for about forty dollars out on Staten Island."

The movie was directed by Armand Mastroianni (actor Marcello's American cousin) and starred Don Scardino and Caitlin O'Heaney. It represented the filmic debut for its thirty-year-old director and was released by MGM/UA. Set in a smalltown suburb of New York City, the film centers on a young bride-to-be, played by O'Heaney, who becomes convinced that someone is watching and following her. The movie has some cinematic sleight-of-hand and a tad more derring-do than you see in most shlock of this ilk, but it is important to remember that these low-budget exploitation flicks can be a springboard for youthful talent.

"I like to do a wide variety of roles," said Hanks. "In repertory, you do that all the time and it eventually becomes fun, playing the prince today and the humble servant tomorrow."

Actually, Hanks did receive notice, although not by name. A New York film critic, in reviewing *He Knows You're Alone*, mentioned that the movie's most inadvertently humorous moment comes at an amusement park "when a college student in Psychology I pompously explains why people like horror movies. 'It's a vicarious thrill,' he says." Even in a tiny walk-on, people were starting to recognize Tom Hanks.

His other role in New York landed him in the lead of a CBS made-for-TV film based on Rona Jaffe's novel, *Mazes and Monsters*, which dealt with the Tolkienish sword-and-sorcery fantasy game that was a then-current fad on some college campuses. On its face, it is an almost exploitative effort which seems stretched out at its 103-minute, feature-length running time. But taken in the Tom Hanks filmography, it is a very revealing artifact.

The story centers around four college classmates from upper-middle-class homes who are sketched out to be misunderstood or plain ignored by their parents. Christopher Makepeace played J.J. Brockway, who we are to believe is a sixteen-year-old genius who's unhappy because his whiz-kid publishing father is never around and his decorator mom keeps redesigning his room. He's lonely and his only friend is a mynah bird who chirps, "Birds don't talk" whenever any-one talks to him. Wendy Crewson portrayed a would-be writer with a case of block and David Wallace appeared as a tow-headed computer brain. Such old warhorses as Susan Strasberg and Vera Miles had small roles as authority figures. The common bond in these kids' lives? They play "Mazes and Monsters," in which they take medieval characters and play-act various power situations based on the psychology of their roles. Into this trio strode Tom Hanks as Robbie Wheeling, look-ing shockingly youthful and acting with amazing straight-facedness, considering the howlingly risible quality of much of the teleplay.

It is a young, still-groping-for-an-acting-persona Hanks that we see in *Mazes and Monsters*, with little of the *savoir-faire* and comic cockiness that would later be associ-ated with him. He was still tentative and un-sure of his sexual appeal. Amazingly enough, this is an asset for the character he plays, who eventually goes over the edge by being unable to distinguish between reality and his "Mazes and Monsters" fantasy.

In the movie, Hanks, who had been an avid player of the game, is seen promising his parents he won't get involved in it again as he starts at a new school after transferring from Tufts. No sooner does he meet pretty Wendy Crewson, though, than Hanks is telling us he's Pardu, the spiritual one, seeking some long-lost brother (father? mother?) who has left and not come back. As he finds himself drawn to Wendy, he also finds himself drawn back into playing the game and dating his partner. There's a charming little scene where Hanks shows her a double bed he's bought so they can move in together on campus, but Wendy inexplicably says he's moving too fast and Tom gets real morose as a result. In his nightmares, he hears the spirit of his dead brother calling to tell him to be celibate and continue pursuing the path to the "Great Hall" and the "Twin Towers." The whole thing ends up with Tom on the roof of—you guessed it—the World Trade Center, threatening to jump off to rejoin his brother in the "Great Hall" beyond.

Absolutely hilarious, of course, except for the fascinating glimpse of Hanks attempting a straightforward dramatic performance, the only one he would have until 1986's Israeli film, *Every Time We Say Goodbye*. The nascent star revealed a great deal, too. His intense spirituality, for one, and his ability to cry and emote. It's all very raw, of course . . . viewers now might almost expect the Hanks of *Bosom Buddies* and *Splash* to pop up and dispel the phony medieval lingo with a single, withering punchline. Yet the character is far more like his pal Peter Scolari describes: "There's two people warring inside Tom, and the one would definitely laugh at and poke fun at the other." In *Mazes and Monsters*, we have a revealing look at that other Hanks, one we definitely would not see again until the emotional breakthrough of *Nothing in Common*.

According to *New York* magazine, it was Hanks's *Mazes and Monsters* role that led to his landing a series of auditions at ABC, to fill parts in various programs the network had in development at the time. The year was 1980.

"I went on the initial 'go-see' with thousands of other people. Basically that consisted of going in, letting these people look at you, and chatting for about a minute and a half. Well, that progressed to sitting in a room chatting for about three minutes, which progressed to reading something from the actual pilot of the show and then making a videotape of that. The next thing I knew I was flying to Los Angeles and reading for the pilot of a show about a couple of guys who dress in drag in order to move into a women's hotel."

That pilot was for *Bosom Buddies*, a show put together by Paramount Television and the same production team responsible for *Laverne and Shirley*. It had been earmarked for ABC's fall 1980 programming lineup.

"In New York I never thought of myself as an artist that was going to be on film or TV," he said to the *Los Angeles Herald Examiner*. "I thought that if I was going to make a living it was going to be in regional theater. Living in New York part of the year and working in places like Louisville, Minneapolis, and Chicago."

The ABC-TV "cattle call" audition in New York—where Hanks's talent manifested itself early on—changed all that. It only took a month before he was winging it out to the Coast, where he read for parts in a flock of new series being planned. He was offered *Bosom Buddies* even though that wasn't one of the series he'd originally read for.

"I had no idea what I was getting into; if somebody had told me, I would probably have choked. Really."

What Tom Hanks didn't know was that the

show had him cast without anyone lined up to play opposite him. Executive producer Chris Thompson explained why he picked Hanks.

"He was funnier than anyone else," he said matter-of-factly. "Which is what I look for when casting a comedy." He also had no idea Hanks would go from the series to superstardom. "You don't put 'star' around his name," he said laconically. "He has sort of an *unusual* face."

Unusual face or not, the show's coproducer Ian Praiser also knew a talent when he saw one.

"The first day I saw him on the set, I thought, 'Too bad he won't be in television for long.' I knew he'd be a movie star in two years."

He wasn't off by much.

"Doing *Bosom Buddies* was like my undergraduate training as an actor," Hanks said. "It was like going to an airplane factory day in and day out. You go into this big hangar and build a plane, and every Friday, it has to fly. Sometimes the wings fall off, but other times, it breaks the sound barrier. And that's what it was like for thirty-eight shows and two years."

3   The *Bosom Buddies* Experience: Some Like It Hot

"What you saw in *Bosom Buddies* is, in many ways, what Tom Hanks is really like."
—Leonard Ripps, producer/story consultant,
Bosom Buddies

"He's about the same on-screen as he is in your living room."
—David Chambers, story editor,
Bosom Buddies

Television stardom is a different kind of animal than silver-screen, cinematic stardom. The weekly requirements of a series sitcom and intimacy of the home setting demand the performers to be somewhat smaller, rather than larger than life.

"People don't want incredibly eccentric characters in their home," says Leonard Ripps, thirty-seven-year-old producer and story consultant for *Bosom Buddies*. "The most important thing for a television actor is his likability. You can't pretend to be likable. You either are or you aren't. I don't know anyone that wouldn't want to have Peter [Scolari] and Tom as friends. If you were twenty-two, wouldn't you have loved to live next door to them?"

The idea for *Bosom Buddies* came from executive producers Edward K. Milkis, Thomas L. Miller, William Boyett, and Chris Thompson, the latter of whom developed the concept from a story line suggested by the others. The germ of the plot was simple. Two young advertising executives, fresh from their midwestern hometown, arrive in New York City, only to find their apartment in the path of a wrecking ball. Stymied about where to relocate, the two are convinced by a female colleague in their office to try the residence hotel she lives in. Of course, the one catch is—shades of *Some Like It Hot*—it's restricted to women. And so, our two heroes make the simple decision to don drag and move in.

Milkis, Miller, Boyett, and Thompson were veterans of sitcoms like *Laverne and Shirley;*

Thompson had just left another series, *Good Time Girls,* about four women sharing a Washington, D.C. boarding house in 1942, a *Swing Shift*-type situation comedy which had originally been called *The Home Front.* Ironically, one of its principals was a young New Rochelle, New York-born actor named Peter Scolari.

Thompson joined the fledgling *Bosom Buddies* team and brought over several of the writers he had worked with on the show, Leonard Ripps and David Chambers, to develop the concept. According to Scolari, neither he nor Hanks were the producers' first choice for the roles they ended up playing. Bobby DeCicco (who was in *1941* and *I Wanna Hold Your Hand*) turned down the Tom Hanks part while Perry Lang (who went on to do *Jocks*) didn't work out as the character eventually played by Scolari. In a pressure-cooker situation a week before they were set to shoot the pilot, Chris Thompson called in his *Good Time Girls* cast member Peter Scolari just for that occasion. Luckily for Scolari, when the show was picked up for distribution by Paramount Television, he was able to join the team.

The concept of two guys in drag was, of

course, as old as show business itself, but the youthful enthusiasm of Hanks and Scolari breathed new life into hoary clichés. It immediately became apparent that there was something special about these two, a comedy pairing of uncommon timing.

"Chris Thompson had experience writing that kind of 'buddy' stuff from his days at *Laverne and Shirley*," says Ripps. "But it was clear Tom and Peter were hitting it off and having fun."

Right from the start, Hanks and Scolari tried to top one another with ad-libs, and that camaraderie came through loud and clear, even on tiny television screens.

"They made up a lot of business," says Ripps about the duo's repartee. "They were very active in suggesting ideas because they're very creative guys. The drag was the most difficult part of the show. They tolerated it for a season. It's just a problem doing a half hour of drag every week. It took a long time getting them in and out of wardrobe, which meant it was tough maintaining any kind of momentum in front of a live audience."

Hanks and Scolari played the roles of Kip Wilson and Henry Desmond, a pair of pre-Yuppie advertising executives who worked

at a Madison Avenue agency called Living-
ston, Gentry & Mishkin. Hanks is the art director and Scolari is the copywriter and the
two work under Ruth Dunbar, played by veteran character actress Holland Taylor. Big gal
Wendie Jo Sperber is the boys' coworker,
Amy Cassidy, who answers phones at the
office. It is the crush Amy develops on Henry
which leads to the suggestion that the boys
try living at the Susan B. Anthony, a hotel
for women only. The boys initially scoff at
the idea, but when Kip meets Sonny Lumet,
a gorgeous blonde dancer played by Donna
Dixon, he convinces Henry to give it a shot,
and the boys don chiffon dresses for the mas-
querade. For the pilot, Lillian Sinclair, the
ever-vigilant hotel manager, was played by
Edie Adams. She was replaced by Lucille
Benson for the remainder of the series. Telma
Hopkins played the black model Isabelle
Hammond.

Bosom Buddies made its debut on ABC
Television on Thanksgiving night, Thursday,
November 27, 1980, to very little fanfare. It
was slotted in the desirable position between
Mork and Mindy and *Barney Miller* at 8:30,
preempting *Laverne and Shirley*. The show

placed seventh in that week's Nielsen rat-
ings, and its future looked bright. The week
after, *Bosom Buddies* ranked just outside the
Top Ten, but for the third week, ABC inexplicably took the show off the air for a network hiatus. "When they brought us back,
we never got those numbers again," says
Scolari ruefully. "The people couldn't find us."
The show went through four time-slot changes
in an attempt to find its audience.

Meanwhile, the critical reaction was tepid
at first.

The *Los Angeles Times* said, "If there was
ever a turkey, this is it . . . [there are] lots of
opportunities for flocks of good-looking chicks
in very few clothes to cluster around at hen
parties, causing all sorts of roguish double
entendres—sort of like *Some Like It Hot*. In
fact you could call this *Some Like It Not* and
include me."

Variety was only slightly more kind: "*Buddies* was sharper and wittier than one has a
right to expect. Nevertheless, the key to this
kind of humor is the flair of the performers—
and Peter Scolari and Tom Hanks get a good
chemistry going between them . . . despite
the plot premise, the concept is broad enough

to be more than a one-joke affair and one hopes its creators are shrewd enough not to overdo its obvious gimmick."

Of course, the creators of the show themselves knew the drag concept wouldn't hold up, but they had, in Hanks and Scolari, a pair of inspired cutups who were beginning to receive some critical attention.

Time said, "*Some Like It Hot* this is not, and some of the jokes are more than nine days old. But there is promise here: The young stars, Tom Hanks and Peter Scolari, know when to underplay a line and when to run with it."

TV Guide also singled out the show's young stars for attention: "Watching these two mince around in frocks is most of the fun in this little pastiche, but the boys are funny about it. Scolari in his Hildegarde disguise is a dithery dear who says 'clappy as a ham,' when she means 'happy as a clam.' Hanks in his Buffy getup is more like a female moose in distress and even more preposterous. The idea that anyone could be fooled by their female impersonations requires a prodigious suspension of disbelief, but I'll make the effort if you will."

Indeed, the first sight of Tom Hanks as

Buffy Wilson and Peter Scolari as Hildegarde Desmond is a great moment in television sitcom history, as the two sashay out of the bathroom half in drag, crooning "Macho Man" in unison. What made Tom and Peter so successful in this show is that they managed to turn nerdiness into a hip quality by being so quick on their feet. As Lenny Ripps put it, "These were not the kind of guys who were on the football team. They were basically eggheads."

Bosom Buddies ran for two seasons on ABC, 1980–81 and 1981–82; a total of thirty-seven episodes and one pilot. While critics agreed that the show's basic drag concept remained a drag, they came to appreciate the razor-sharp timing developed by young Hanks and Scolari. Each show often became a "can you top this?" with the two young actors ad-libbing up a storm. The show's theme song, Billy Joel's "My Life," set the tone. Hanks and Scolari were the prototypes for today's Yuppies. They are seen in the montage credit sequence in a variety of settings . . . tripping over one another while playing softball in the park, buying hot dogs from a street vendor, tanning on the street while putting coins in a meter nearby . . . you name it.

"We were aiming for a slightly hipper audience than your standard sitcom," says Lenny Ripps, and indeed the repartee, not only between Hanks and Scolari, but with the rest of the cast, was certainly more pointed than what is usually found on your average TV series. There was constant wisecracking about current events, both highbrow and lowbrow culture, as well as frequent references to music and sports, including Hanks's beloved Cleveland Browns and Indians. In the very first episode, there are references to reading Sylvia Plath and *Black Like Me*, which came up when Hanks and Scolari first consider donning drag to move into the hotel. There are also great lines like Hanks murmuring, "Is anybody else getting real warm?" when Donna Dixon enters the room; or Scolari looking skyward and winking, "Good job, God," when Dixon sashays in wearing leotards.

After putting on women's clothes for the first time, Hanks beams, "I feel like a completely different kind of man," to which Scolari responds, "Take off the dress." When Scolari chides Hanks about his infatuation with Donna Dixon, saying, "She thinks you're a girl," Hanks retorts with a line worthy of Joe

E. Brown's immortal "Well, nobody's perfect" in *Some Like It Hot:* "I'll settle. . . . "

When the drag angle became, as expected, stale—both actors were not too happy about changing back and forth in front of the live studio audience—people suddenly started concentrating on Hanks's and Scolari's comic gifts, not to mention those of their talented costars. Holland Taylor, as the guys' love-crazed older ad agency boss, played the Betty White mother confessor perfectly, with many good punchlines. Donna Dixon was the archetypal dumb blonde, but she brought a lot of flair and intelligence to the role. Both Telma Hopkins and Wendie Jo Sperber had their share of good rejoinders, too. In all, the writers were pretty generous and by *Bosom Buddies'* second season, the show's two leading lights were recognized as true talents, even out of dresses.

By the second season, the show had become a chic cult item, not least because respected television critic James Wolcott had written in the *Village Voice* that he loved the show and considered it a "classic." Pulitzer Prize-winning Howard Rosenberg of the *Los Angeles Times* wrote, "*Bosom Buddies* is a show on the edge of something. It has not yet found its groove. It remains too scatter-shot and uneven. But the groove is in sight . . . Tom Hanks and Peter Scolari are terrific together as best friends Kip Wilson and Henry Desmond, their chemistry so right, their timing so sharp that you'd think they'd been wisecracking together all their lives. Often they are better than their material, with what they say being less amusing than how they say it. . . . One of the nicer things about *Bosom Buddies* is its tender side. It shows men touching without shame and close friends getting emotional about their relationship. . . . "

The second season, in which the boys finally emerge from drag, ranged far and wide in story ideas and situations. In one episode, Tom and Peter have a flashback at a high school reunion and go back to their teenage years, with Hanks as a drug-addled hippie and Scolari as the straightlaced hall monitor. The gist of the story is Peter's turndown of a deaf classmate's invitation to the prom and meeting the same woman years later at the reunion. It is a touching and hilarious flashback, worthy in its way as a miniature *Peggy Sue Got Married*. Or the episode in which

Tom and Peter organize a cable special in order to get a rat poison account, the highlight turning out to be Wendie Jo Sperber's Carmen Miranda routine, not to mention Scolari and Hanks as jugglers.

"We tried to have fun with the form of the show," says Lenny Ripps. "We felt there were plenty of stories in two young guys trying to make it in the business world. The strengths of the show were in the performances and the jokes. You're allowed to be as crazy as you want in sitcoms as long as you have a moral attached.

"Tom and Peter kept the material fresh every day. Because they were new in the business, you didn't go through the bullshit you get from the more established actors. Their egos and vanity hadn't evolved yet."

Or as Peter Scolari insists, "It was the happiest set in Hollywood."

Tom Hanks came into his own in *Bosom Buddies.* It was more than just applying the craft he had so painstakingly learned in repertory and by performing Shakespeare. His quick wit and ebullient spirits came from an innate ability to adapt to the situation, part and parcel of the experiences he'd had due to his chaotic home life. On *Bosom Buddies,* he rediscovered the extended family he must have craved, precisely that camaraderie which had appealed to him when he first joined the theater. He also developed a style of humor all his own, what Lenny Ripps calls "tony, rich kid's comedy.

"Although he was serious about his job, Tom had fun acting. What he's selling is that kind of glib, *Harvard Lampoon*, upper-crust comedy. Most of the writing before the *Lampoon* came from comedy writers who grew up poor. It was self-effacing. . . .

"Tom is very funny, but you have no idea who he is. You don't have a glimpse into his inner being because everything becomes an excuse for a joke. I think Tom Hanks is most successful when he tries to be sincere, like he was in *Splash* or *Nothing in Common*. When he comes off like a spoiled rich kid, like he did in *Volunteers*, the audience won't buy it, no matter how funny he is. The kind of comedy in *Bosom Buddies* doesn't bare the soul like the traditional style. But just because Tom is a private person, don't confuse that with cold. Tom Hanks doesn't hide things . . . he just doesn't talk about personal matters. Which I think is a significant distinction."

"What you see is pretty much what you

get with Tom," says his good buddy David Chambers. "There was a certain amount of competition between Tom and Peter but I think it was of the creative kind, which is valuable. Tom is always wide open. He's always confident. Even when he's highly energized, he seems relaxed. I think that's really important in acting, film acting in particular, where your face is forty feet high on the big screen. I don't get the feeling Tom is acting so much as projecting his own personality in whatever his part is, which is the essence of good movie acting."

Lenny Ripps feels Hanks's naturalness is the key to his success.

"Most of the successful television actors play extensions of themselves on camera," he says. "They are essentially who they are, which is not quite as important in film. Like, you have no idea who Dustin Hoffman is, but you don't need to. You don't see him in your living room every week, but you see a film he's in maybe once every two or three years. All you need to know is the character he's playing. The pressure is such in a weekly series that the actors show you exactly who they are. In many ways, those characters played by Tom and Peter are exactly who they are. Because who they are comes out in their parts. Tom Hanks was really flip and glib and Peter was really romantic and emotional. Take almost any popular television show and you'll see the main performers are not that dissimilar off camera. There was a genuine sense of enjoyment that came through in their acting. And that's something you can't write or create.

"Unlike the old comics, these guys didn't turn their humor back at themselves. They were confident about who they were. It wasn't like the traditional humor that makes fun of yourself. These guys were too sure of themselves for that, without coming off as cocky. . . . "

The teaming of Tom Hanks and Peter Scolari was certainly something special. A young Tom had found a kindred spirit and used the occasion to hone his skills to a fine edge. *Bosom Buddies* was, in retrospect, the perfect vehicle for Hanks's talents and a once-in-a-lifetime showcase. But it was still just a television sitcom, and a failed television sitcom at that. For, after the end of the show's second season, ABC canceled *Bosom Buddies*. The final show aired on August 5, 1982, and the program, despite its growing following (and over 35,000 letters of protest), was history.

"The television show had come out of nowhere," said Tom Hanks's best buddy, Tom Lizzio. "Then out of nowhere, it got canceled. He figured he'd be back to pulling ropes and hanging lights in a theater."

Indeed, Hanks's confidence was given a jolt by the demise of *Bosom Buddies*. He appeared in a variety of guest shots on other television series during this time, including spots on *Family Ties*, where he had a recurring role as Meredith Baxter Birney's alcoholic brother, Ned O'Donnell; *Taxi*; and *Happy Days*.

It was on *Happy Days*—where he played a guy pushed by Fonzie out of a swing during childhood only to return as a black belt karate expert bent on revenge—that Hanks made a connection that was to play an important role in his future. While filming that episode of the program, he met series costar Ronnie Howard.

"Tom was just hysterically funny and made a lasting impression," said Ron. That impression remained when Howard was set to cast a movie he'd been working on. About a mermaid, it was called *Splash*. Landing the male lead was another big break for Tom Hanks, the one that would put him on the road to motion picture stardom and raise his salary from the $9,000 an episode he received for *Bosom Buddies* (a lot of money for a guy who'd been starving in Shakespeare) to well over $1 million for a film.

4 A Match Made in Comedy Heaven: Hanks & Scolari

"*Bosom Buddies* was great because it made us very fast. The whole thing was delivering the goods as best you could. If you couldn't deliver them good, you had to deliver them bad, as long as you delivered them. It's flying by the seat of your pants. You ask as many questions as you can, but eventually, it's 'never mind, just do it.' You can't be lazy. It became our whole life. We did so much of it in such a short period of time, it all blends. . . . "

—Tom Hanks

After Vincent Dowling, the director of the Great Lakes Shakespeare Festival in Cleveland and the man who first gave a young Tom Hanks the confidence to believe he could be an actor, perhaps the next most important figure in our hero's creative evolution would be his *Bosom Buddies* costar Peter Scolari. Only two years apart in age and both blessed with quick wit and nimble minds, Hanks and Scolari became "bosom buddies" their very first day on the set.

"There was an immediate professional connection," recalls Scolari on the set of *The Newhart Show*, where he plays Michael Harris, recently called "the biggest jerk on television" by David Letterman. "Tom and I started winging the script from moment one. We were ad-libbing from the beginning. The chemistry was born. Later that afternoon, we became fast friends. And it happened on just that time scale. We liked each other right away. I was always two years older than Tom, so I was like his older brother. I pointed him in the direction of the camera and he handled himself very well."

Peter Scolari was born September 12, 1954 in New Rochelle, New York, to an attorney father who was an All-American football player and a social worker/psychologist mother. He was always a precocious lad, like Tom himself.

"My mother tells me I was always this serious," he told *TV Guide*. "That when I was two, I was having arguments with her saying, 'No, no, that's not what Descartes meant at all.'"

At a very early age, he stole the first scene of *Peer Gynt* with a pratfall and used to crack up his third-grade classmates with impressions of John F. Kennedy.

"My parents would bring me out of bed and say, 'That's our kid,'" remembers Peter.

He attended Edgemont High School in Scarsdale, New York, and spent a year at Occidental College outside of Los Angeles before returning to New York to become a founding member of the Colonnades Theater Lab, where he spent "six and a half years with a bunch of maniacs," among whom were eventual stars like Jeff Goldblum, Michael O'Keefe, and Danny DeVito.

A three-sport man who takes after his athletic dad in physical dexterity, Scolari is also an adept juggler and can run the 100 in 9.9 seconds. At Colonnades, his first public performance was not juggling but in a play called *Reflections* in 1975, for which he received plaudits from no less than the *New York Times*. Like his future buddy Hanks, Scolari learned everything there was to know about the theater, and found sustenance in the extended repertory family.

After moving out to Hollywood in 1980, Peter landed a number of bit parts in television series like *Struck by Lightning*, *Out of the Blue*, *The Further Adventures of Wally Brown*, and *Angie*, the latter of which featured soon-to-be-colleague Leonard Ripps as a writer. He had a regular role as Benny in *Good Time Girls* when that show was canceled, allowing him to take the part in the *Bosom Buddies* pilot, just when he'd been ready to return to New York and his wife, a criminal defense lawyer named Lisa Kretszchmar.

"I told my friends in New York, 'I'm coming home, I've done my Hollywood thing, got a lot of money, now it's back to the theater . . . unh, not so fast. . . .'"

The *Bosom Buddies* producers had been desperate. When they were set to film a pilot and the chemistry between the show's leads just did not happen, Chris Thompson thought of a talented young actor he'd worked with on *Good Time Girls* and gave Peter a ring.

The pilot was shot, but came in about eight to ten minutes too long, which meant it had to be trimmed.

"It was the funniest television show I had ever seen," reminisces Peter. "But they had to cut ten minutes out of it, which is death. There was no logic left."

Not that there was a whole lot to begin with. From the get-go, Hanks and Scolari raised this tepid little one-joke sitcom to the rarified levels of fine, absurd farce.

"Everything you saw that you liked about *Bosom Buddies* was very carefully discussed between Tom and myself," insists Scolari. "We planned everything. I don't think there could be a closer team than we were. It wasn't like [Tony] Randall and [Jack] Klugman [in *The Odd Couple* TV series] or other greats of the past, who did it professionally. We did it quite personally. We spent a tremendous amount of personal time together."

Indeed, the two young actors were in much the same situation. Both were experiencing a taste of success and recognition for the first time . . . and both had left a loved one behind in New York City while they toiled in the day-to-day insanity of a weekly network series.

"It was hard," says Peter. "When I first started doing the show, it was a very troubling time for my first wife. All of a sudden, this actor who she loved and who worked mostly off- and off-off-Broadway and was someone she admired for his acting becomes overnight a media figure, and she couldn't cope with that. I was twenty-six years old then so I couldn't exactly cope with it either. So, I didn't. I shied away. I didn't appear on talk shows. I didn't get a publicist or do interviews. Because I felt I got to that point on my acting ability and I wanted to protect that reputation of being an actor, not a media figure."

So Hanks and Scolari were inevitably drawn to one another. Scolari discounts the conventional wisdom that what you see on-screen with Tom is what you get.

"I've known that's not true from day one," he says, "when we sat down and talked about our fathers in the studio commissary. I realized right away this was a tremendously sensitive guy, a very family-oriented guy. He's a good father and a good man. He runs very, very deep and even those who enjoyed him in *Nothing in Common* as much as I did have only glimpsed the tip of this actor's depth. He has something which is sorely missing in this town and that is a depth of character and dignity inside he's never out of touch with. He's like the circus clown who runs as deep as you can get, but you never know it because of the frivolity in his day-to-day existence."

The off-camera camaraderie was translated into an on-camera genuineness that couldn't be faked. The relationship was real, and the banter took off from there.

"The writers were real good at setting up the feel of improvisation," says Peter of the repartee. "We only ad-libbed twenty percent of the material, which is about one hundred percent more than you'll find in most sitcoms."

The two were never happy with the show's main cross-dressing concept, though.

"Neither of us liked it at all," says Peter. "I think it speaks well of our professionalism that we did the very best we could. We tried to make it better than we thought it was, better than we thought it had a right to be. We didn't think it belonged in the show, actually. After awhile, we just wanted to get out of it. We had used it to establish the premise of the show and it was time to move on. We wanted to play on our chemistry without the drag. But, according to ABC demographic research, that was the element the audience liked the best, so go figure."

While the show's premise came from *Some Like It Hot*, Scolari insists the two wanted their performances only to allude to the original's Jack Lemmon and Tony Curtis, not mimic them.

"I don't want to compare Tom and I to [*The Honeymooners'*] Norton and Kramden, because they *were* the greatest, so don't misunderstand me. But, just as Jackie Gleason and Art Carney knew they were playing Laurel and Hardy, they didn't want their audience to know that. Everyone knew we were playing Lemmon and Curtis. We took some things there. I thought Lemmon had this beautiful quality of trying to act womanly, while Curtis would crack jokes and be obvious about being in drag. My character, Henry, was the soulful half of the pair. He almost believed he was a woman at times. Like in that episode where Buffy and Hildegarde go to a singles bar and I ask, 'Is it too much to ask some hunk to come over and buy me a drink or show me some tenderness?' and Kip as Buffy goes, 'C'mon Henry, Rin Tin Tin, calm down, boy.'"

Because the reviews had been mostly negative, the *Bosom Buddies* producers and writers continued to tinker with the show to find the correct formula. The show was renewed for a second season by the skin of its teeth.

"That show was not a job to us, it was our lives; we worked harder than anything. We were there until eleven or midnight if it wasn't as good as we wanted," remembers Peter.

It wasn't enough, though. "As Tom said, we were the show that wouldn't die," says Peter, who insists that by the time the cancellation finally came, "it didn't rankle us in the slightest. By the end of that second year, we felt, 'If you're not going to love us, get rid of us.' Because to be funny, jazzy, and clever, week in and week out, it takes a toll on you mentally, like having to throw a dart in the same place over and over. The network is more sorry than we were; ABC executives have come up to me in the supermarket and apologized."

Looking back at *Bosom Buddies*, it is easy to realize the show's two archetypal Yuppie heroes actually prefigured that now-clichéd term, predicting the rise of the white-collar baby boomers wanting in to the good life.

"The word didn't exist at the time," agrees Peter. "Henry and Kip were very upfront about having material values. There was even one episode where we discussed whether it was all worth it to get some big account we had just landed. And the upshot was, at least we were still friends. We had each other. I think that's what the Yuppies are missing today . . . that commitment, that friendship."

Unfortunately, the strain of doing the series eventually caused Peter and his wife to split apart. The strain due to the breakup of his marriage, coinciding with the demise of the show, hurt Peter in trying to get roles after *Bosom Buddies*. While Tom Hanks, fresh from an on-camera romance with Donna Dixon, walked right into leading-man parts, it was difficult for Peter to make a similar transition.

"I'm just a renowned nice guy," he complains amiably. "And nice guys finish third. With two friends like the guys on *Bosom Buddies*, you needed one to be the reasonable one, the soulful one. And I clearly saw that as my task. In some of the show's best episodes, we flipflopped the format. And then Kip would offer some heart-to-heart advice to Henry. And that is not unlike our friendship in real life. I was always a little older and a little more experienced. I would fight the bigger battles with the executive producer about the script.

"We thought we were the first of the nice-guy comedy teams. We insisted on not slapping one another or causing physical harm.

We made fun of ourselves. We knew we were a pair of bimbos and idiots. And our humor was a form of defense, protection."

Those defenses didn't work for Peter. With the end of his TV show and his marriage, Scolari was "heartbroken, in a very dispirited, unhappy place." He went on some auditions, but didn't land anything until he got a role in a series called *And Baby Makes Five,* in which he played an accountant with three children whose wife unexpectedly gives birth to twins. It didn't last long, and, combined with his former buddy Tom Hanks's feature film success in the 1984 *Splash,* it pushed Scolari further into a funk.

"A lot of writers were asking me why I wasn't as big a star as Tom," he says now. "And, truth be told, it did hurt, but then I asked myself, What is it that hurts? That your good friend has a great job? That you have a nice job, but it's not in as high profile an arena? What is it that hurts? And I finally came to grips with the fact that it didn't hurt, that it *affected* me, but it didn't hurt. Why should Tom's success hurt me? It has nothing to do with me. I'm happy for Tom. The relationship I've had with him has always been too solid and too honest for that kind of envy.

What other people want to think or believe is their privilege. I make a joke about it.

"Where Tommy is—and he deserves to be there—is a wonderful place, but he's paying a tremendous price for it, too. He's got to get the next good movie. I don't. But the real measure of success here is if you're content with what you're doing. If everything is happening in its right time. And, for me, it's been pushed on by Tommy's success and that bizarre light which has been refracted my way and asks, 'Well, what about you?' And I asked, Well, what about me and I started asking the questions. What did it mean to me? If you asked Tom three or four years ago which one of us would become big in films, he'd have gone, 'Oh Scolari, for sure . . . and I just hope he brings me along. . . . ' He was probably as shocked as anyone at his own success with *Splash*. He told me, 'I'm gonna do this Ron Howard thing; I hope it doesn't embarrass me.' So you don't know.

"The real measure of success has got to be that there's this guy out there just as talented as I am and as talented as Tom is and he's doing five lines on a soap opera this week. Is he any less successful than Tom or I? You begin to understand perspective, which is everything in Hollywood. You've got to be strong, to bear up under pressure and the 'attack of the hype people.' Perhaps the guy with the five lines in the soap opera is more successful than Tom or I have been in bearing up under that pressure. Because he's happy, he's content. He knows his time will come, just as surely as my time will come. And Tommy's will come, over and over again.

"That's what I've learned over the last two years. I've come into my own and, if the industry hasn't exactly recognized that, a part of it certainly has. I have the respect of the people I work with. We enjoy one another. Tom came by last year to see us shoot a couple of episodes of *The Newhart Show* and he had the time of his life. He said, almost truthfully, 'This is great. I miss this.' And I told him, 'Don't miss it, because you are where you belong.'

"I belong being Tom Poston's friend on *The Newhart Show* right now. My personal growth is in a good place. I'm not afraid and I know someone in Tom's position has to be a little afraid because the stakes are so high. That's the nature of the business. You're on top now, but who knows what's gonna be six months from now? Sly Stallone is probably the biggest star around right now and I wouldn't cast him in a high school play, so is he a success? As a media figure or a movie star, yes. As an actor? Ask Tom Hanks what five actors he respects the most and I'll be one of them, and the same with me and him. On the level he and I relate, we're equally successful."

There was a time when Peter didn't handle the situation with such equanimity, though. A little glimpse of that came on a recent Scolari appearance on *The David Letterman Show*, where he responded to a question from Letterman—as to whether he ever talked to Tom—with a joke about how Hanks's secretary puts him on hold.

"I don't think Tommy would respect me if I didn't make that joke," he says. "I still regard him as a younger brother. His people and my people never talk; *we* do. That's just the style of Letterman's show and I felt I had to take a shot at Tom, since it was the first time I'd been on the program and he's been on several times. That was a comment on the nature of the industry more than it is about our friendship. I feel, if I needed Tom for something, he would be there, and I think he feels that way about me. Neither of us are Hollywood types."

In fact, Scolari insists that stardom hasn't affected the Tom Hanks he knows.

"He's had to carry more sensitivity to what's going on around him, by the nature of who he is," explains Peter. "If anything, he's happy with his success, but, being a bright man, he's troubled by fame's pitfalls. He knows that your friendships and lifestyles change and these are legitimate threats to the regularity of who you really are.

"It depends on the individual. My particular feeling is, if you have the unyielding ambition to be a star, it's probably your way of finding an identity. That can be a terrible trap. From my experience, stars have very fragile identities. They barely exist as people. But that hasn't afflicted Tom . . . nor I."

As for whether his quick success is responsible for his current separation, Peter refuses to speculate.

"You can't deny the fact that with success comes tremendous pressure," he says. "And a responsibility to bear up under that pressure."

Despite Peter's closeness with Tom, there

were sides to Hanks that not even Scolari knew existed, including at least one real shocker.

"I had known Tom for about a year and he confided to me that he was real religious in high school, a biblical fanatic," says Peter. "'Believe it or not,' he told me once, 'I was the kind of guy who'd walk up to you in the hallways and say, "Listen, no pressure or anything, but later on, after school, I'm going to have a couple of guys over the house to talk about the Bible and, if you wanna come by, you're welcome."' And I was floored. It was a revelation to me. 'Then, you're a re-formed Jesus freak?' I asked him. And he said yeah. I thought, 'Gee, I thought I knew you.'

"That's when I started to get a glimpse as to where all that shyness and tenderness in Tom came from . . . and why it's a little bit hidden. Because this is a guy who, if you take the two people that Tom Hanks has been in his life, one of his personalities would make tremendous fun of the other. So, he keeps those sides private. They're for Tom to know about and not for us to probe. Who knows the right equation as to how much of that interior life you should show the public? All

I know is Tom has a very strong desire to probe that serious side of his personality."

Although Tom Hanks wouldn't reveal it until much later in his career, after he'd already established himself as one of the screen's most gifted comics.

5 Making Waves With *Splash:* The Big Breakthrough

"For [John Candy's] brother, we tried to get Michael Keaton, we tried to get John Travolta, tried to get Bill Murray, tried to get Dudley Moore, tried to get Chevy Chase. They were all unavailable or not interested. The word was real good on Tom Hanks around town. He read, and he was terrific. We just stopped looking."
—Ron Howard in *Film Comment,* on casting
Tom Hanks in *Splash*

It wasn't an altogether unlikely scenario placing Tom Hanks in *Splash* as a leading man in his first major motion picture. After all, director Ron Howard had seen his work in *Happy Days*, some of whose producers also worked on *Bosom Buddies*. The fact that *Splash* itself was a success, earning more than $60 million in grosses and $34 million in rentals (according to *Variety* magazine), was far more of a long shot. The movie's critical and financial windfall made stars not only of its director Ron Howard and star Tom Hanks, but of performers Daryl Hannah, John Candy, Eugene Levy, and the writing team of Lowell Ganz and Babaloo Mandel as well.

Splash was the third directorial effort of young actor Ron Howard, known by many as Andy Griffith's young son Opie on the long-running television series, following *Grand Theft Auto* for Roger Corman and *Night Shift,* which costarred Henry Winkler and Michael Keaton. *Splash* was Howard's project from the very start, and the fact that it was even made at all was a triumph—because all along it had been going up against a proposed $30 million fantasy film based on the same topic: a guy falling in love with a mermaid. That project, dubbed *Mermaid,* had such heavyweights as Warren Beatty and Jessica Lange, writer Robert (*Chinatown*) Towne, director Herbert Ross, producer Ray Star, and *E.T.* creator Carlo Rambaldo on hand, and was all set to go when a threatened actors' strike put it on hold.

In the meantime, Howard teamed up with producer Brian Grazer, writer Bruce Jay

Friedman, and writers Babaloo Mandel and Lowell Ganz, who had worked with him on *Happy Days* and *Night Shift.*

"Beatty and those guys didn't build their careers by racing to beat strike deadlines," Howard told *People.* "We, on the other hand, were *happy* to win a footrace."

At that point, the $9 million mermaid epic Howard had in mind took on high-stakes proportions. He had already passed on directing both *Mr. Mom* and *Footloose* (with their combined grosses of over $100 million) to fight for *Splash.* He finally sold the idea to, of all places, Disney Studios, who were looking to launch their new film distribution arm, Touchstone Pictures. It was all too perfect for Ronnie Howard.

"Y'know, little Ronnie Howard grows up to make films for Walt Disney Studios. That bothered me. It seemed counterproductive."

But Disney convinced Howard that they wanted a new adult image for their revamped film company. In fact, *Splash,* with its furtive shots of mermaid Daryl Hannah's bare backside, became the first R-rated film in Walt Disney's history.

"It's great when a studio gambles like that,"

Howard exulted to *People.* "I always go for the underdog."

Howard countered *Mermaid'*s star power with a cast of veritable newcomers. Many of them came from the ranks of television, as Ron did himself. The Duncan, Oklahoma-born Howard made his screen debut at the age of eighteen months in the 1956 western, *Frontier Woman.* He and his brother Clint were in a number of television series and movies. The quintessential freckle-faced lad for eight years on *The Andy Griffith Show,* Howard finally was allowed to break out of the corn-fed mold in George Lucas's *American Graffiti.* Ron enrolled in the University of Southern California's cinema studies program and reluctantly left his classwork in 1975 to star in ABC's *Happy Days* TV series, portraying well-meaning but gullible Richie Cunningham. That show also created a sensation in his sidekick Henry Winkler, better known as "the Fonz." It was a friendship that would continue when the two worked together on the feature film named *Night Shift.*

While he had been directing short 8 mm films since the age of fifteen, Howard convinced producer Roger Corman to let him direct the sequel to a typical car exploitation flick he had acted in, called *Eat My Dust.* The result was *Grand Theft Auto.*

"I hated *Eat My Dust,* but from my film-school days at USC I knew that Roger Corman was like a ray of hope for student filmmakers. He was one guy who would take chances on directors. My father [Rance, also an actor/writer/director/producer] and I had a spec script that we had written, and I went up to Roger and said I'd do *Eat My Dust* if we could do this other script. He read it and said he liked the writing but it wasn't the sort of movie he made. He said if I'd do *Eat My Dust,* he'd guarantee that me and my father could write a story outline, and, if he liked it, we could do it, but I had to be in it. And, if that didn't work out, he'd still guarantee me a second-unit directing job. . . .

"As it happened, *Eat My Dust* was a huge hit and Roger wanted a sequel, so we came up with *Grand Theft Auto,* which is the title that came back in a market research test. He said he wanted me to make a picture, but it had to be a 'car chase comedy, young people on the run' and I had to star in it. Those were the givens. So we adapted a kind of semi-dramatic idea my dad had and made the movie. It clearly wouldn't have been what I would have chosen for my first film, but it turned out to be a great experience for me. I feel that work begets work, and if you can put yourself into the flow, good things will come to you. I just told myself, 'Okay, it's a car crash picture, so I'm going to make it the very best car crash picture that I can.' We shot it in twenty-two days for $602,000 and it grossed around $15 million."

After a series of made-for-TV features, Howard directed his second major movie, *Night Shift*, with his producer/partner, Brian Grazer, who'd started as a clerk in the business affairs department at Warner Brothers while moonlighting as a script reader for Brut/ Faberge Productions. The ambitious youngster quickly made enough connections to find a position as a talent agent, then moved into development and production with Paramount Pictures, where he met Ron Howard. The pair began discussing the possibilities of a film about two young men running a call-girl ring from a city morgue.

"Brian and I were just about the youngest people at Paramount at the time," Howard told *Film Comment*. "The idea for *Night Shift* came from an article in the paper. I had been working with Lowell Ganz and Babaloo Mandel, two writers from *Happy Days*, and they immediately went to work on the story and it was real funny. We made a deal with it. We always got a big kick out of the concept, but I'm not sure that it was a readily accessible idea to a lot of people. . . .

"The frustrating thing about it is it was always such a crowd pleaser. We never had a bad screening. And it did very well on cable. I think that *Night Shift*'s popularity on cable and in videocassette rental helped *Splash* get started."

Indeed, the genesis of *Splash* can be seen in *Night Shift*. The mild-mannered straight lead, played by Henry Winkler, is gradually pushed into a life of zany impulse and danger by a wacky sidekick, in this case Michael Keaton. Ironically, though it is Tom Hanks who plays the straight man to John Candy's cutup in *Splash*, he is most often compared as an actor to wild guy Keaton.

Night Shift had its critical supporters, but *Splash*, with $9 million and a new studio riding on its outcome, was an even bigger test for director Ron Howard and new leading man Tom Hanks.

"Brian Grazer came up with the idea for *Splash* as he had with *Night Shift*," said Ron. "He was driving along the Pacific Coast Highway, thinking about mermaids, and he thought that would make a good comedy. He worked on it awhile and put it into development at United Artists with Bruce Jay Friedman doing the draft, and then another writer came on who didn't get screen credit. The script got put into turnaround just about the time we were finishing up *Night Shift*. Brian handed me the script and said if I wanted to get involved with it, I could.

"Once again I had to talk myself into making a picture. I wasn't sure I wanted to do another comedy after *Night Shift*, an almost silly comedy. But I started thinking about the romantic possibilities of the project, and we came up with a new structure. Lowell and Babaloo did a one-page rewrite and it became a character comedy, more of a love story. There was too much time spent underwater in the first draft. There was this kind of underwater kingdom with scenes, dialogue, and jokes, and it was not going to be believable. Now, it's mostly above water and it's really the guy's point of view. We had nothing to lose. We were the underdogs. The people at Disney were the only ones to believe in us. They liked our script. . . . "

For a film about a mermaid and some true *Three Stooges*-styled slapstick comedy, *Splash* succeeded with audiences because it became what Ron Howard set out to make—a believable, touching love story with feelings dominating rather than special effects. And first-time leading man Tom Hanks had quite a lot to do with that believability.

Hanks plays Allen Bauer, the straightlaced young businessman who falls in love with the mermaid embodied by Daryl Hannah. One of *Splash*'s most successful gambits in establishing its elegiac mood is its pre-opening credit flashback to the momentous occasion when an eight-year-old Allen jumps off a Cape Cod ferry to join a beckoning mermaid, only to nearly drown and end up back on the boat surrounded by concerned passengers. We see his chubby older brother Freddie, character already firmly established, dropping coins on the pretense of looking up the lady passengers' skirts.

With a quick cut to the present, Allen Bauer is now grownup and a partner with his brother in the family-run wholesale produce market.

Freddie, a fat satyr in white scarves, is still looking up women's skirts. Like the team of Hanks and Scolari, the team of Hanks and SCTV alumni John Candy is an inspired flip-flop of straightman and wiseguy.

"The two aren't remotely conceivable as brothers," wrote David Denby in a *New York* magazine review of the movie. "Hanks is slender and dark, with curly hair and crinkly eyes, while Candy, a roaring tub of guts, looks like a lascivious Charles Laughton throwing Christians to the lions in *The Sign of the Cross.* But the implausibility is itself funny, and the two men complement each other. Hanks, a TV and theater actor, is an expert comic, with steel springs in his legs, but he's also good-looking and relaxed enough to be a leading man. He commands the emotional center of his scenes, holding your sympathy in place, while Candy, a libidinous blonde bull, frightening to behold, frolics madly at the edges."

On the set Hanks, a big SCTV fan, admitted he was in awe of his costar at first.

"John and I have developed a surprising dual relationship," said Tom. "And it's not at all competitive or 'can you top this?' It has been, from the beginning, 'What shall we do here?' John is a pacer—he'll start pacing around and he'll say, 'What if we try this?' By the time we get to actually doing it, it's a meshing of gears that makes some pretty good music. John is an ambassador of goodwill. I've never met a guy as sweet and giving. I don't pal around with him off camera, but the things that he thinks are funny also crack me up. He also knows how to improvise from his days with Second City. We're striving for the same end result, to be funny and interesting and to get the audience involved."

"The great thing about Tom is his size," Candy, who went on to costar with Hanks in *Volunteers,* told *Rolling Stone* in its 1986 year-end issue. "He's smaller than I am. This, for me, is a plus in a working situation, as I can usually get my own way in whatever scene we are working on by intimidation or sheer force. I don't normally go in for bully tactics, but in the movie business, it's every man for himself. Tom is also a very funny and decent human being, as well as a good friend."

At first, Howard thought Hanks would play Freddie, but quickly changed his mind when he saw that the actor was capable of playing a tender role.

"Tom had to be serious and poignant, as well as romantic and vulnerable," Ron said.

"There were moments when he had to be funny, not to mention the difficult scenes where he had to act underwater. I think of him as a terrific leading man, like Jack Lemmon or James Stewart—funny guys who make you care."

Producer Grazer says the part of Allen wasn't easy to cast. "The character was funny but not quirky. Most comedians have a cute idiosyncratic quality. We didn't want that. Tom is warm. Men like him. Women like him. But it was odd. There he was with everything at stake. And his career was stalled. They wouldn't even let him read for *Police Academy*. But he walked into the audition in jeans, construction boots, and a workshirt. I've seen thousands of actors read for parts, and I've never seen anyone who looked as if he felt as comfortable with himself."

Before giving him the part that would change his life, Grazer asked him if he did standup comedy and Hanks replied, "No, I don't do standup. I'm a chickenshit. Give me something written down and I think I can make it funny. But don't tell me to get up there and be funny."

He got the role.

Splash spent seventeen days of principal

photography on location in New York City, filming at landmarks such as the Statue of Liberty (where the mermaid first steps ashore bone-naked, to the delight and astonishment of the tourists in one of the movie's most famous scenes), the Museum of Natural History and its renowned whale room, Bloomingdale's department store (where Daryl as the mermaid Madison cracks all the TV sets and Hanks replies to the stunned salesperson, "How about those Knicks?"), and Columbus Circle. The production then moved to Los Angeles for additional filming at locations throughout southern California before traveling to the Bahamas for the underwater sequences, which lasted another sixteen days. Those dangerous shots proved a challenge for Hanks.

"I found myself pounding on my chest, which was the hand signal for 'I need air,'" joked Tom to *People* about making the movie. "I grew up in awe of Jacques Cousteau and the *American Sportsman* shows. Scuba was something I would maybe do on a dare after enough beers. But as a job I found the diving a real challenge."

The best part, of course, was kissing lovely Daryl Hannah at thirty feet below.

"You still hold your breath, still close your eyes. Same old stuff. She was so natural and giving. She made it easy to act like I loved her."

Lovely Daryl Hannah, daughter of a wealthy owner of a Chicago tugboat and barge company, had already had a number of small film and TV roles (notably as the replicant in *Blade Runner* and as part of the *menage à trois* in Randal Kleiser's little-seen *Summer Lovers*), but *Splash* was her big breakthrough, just as it was for Hanks. The two have become forever etched in people's minds through *Splash*, but Tom denied there was ever anything more than a professional relationship.

"Daryl and I are quite happy," he joked to a reporter from *Cosmopolitan* who insisted young film fans thought the two were married. "She's very quiet, kind of mysterious, not given over to any cartoony histrionics. Daryl shows up and does the job."

Splash opened in theaters on March 9, 1984, to almost uniformly good reviews. The *New York Times* said, "*Splash* could have been shorter, but it probably couldn't have been much sweeter."

Variety extoled, ". . . a charming mermaid yarn notable for winning suspension of belief and fetching byplay between Daryl Hannah and Tom Hanks . . . whose desperate vulnerability is on the mark."

New York magazine put it succinctly: "It's been a long time since we've had a good boy-meets-fish story, and *Splash* is a fairly irresistible one."

The movie swam out of the theaters a success. Hanks told *People*, "I didn't think it would be a stinker, maybe a little cartoonish, but the first weekend I get a call, 'Six million bucks at the box office.' You're in your first big film. It's beyond my comprehension. That's a lot of money. You can't get it much better, right outta the box. It's perfect."

When asked if scripts were starting to come in, he replied, "Yes, the deluge has begun. There is an immediate rush to get me all sorts of scripts with no financing."

As for whether his friends treated him differently, he joked, "They ask to get in for free. Sorry, guys. I didn't have points in *Splash*. The last time they gave an actor points I think was Fess Parker for Davy Crockett."

In its first seventeen days of release, *Splash* took in $24 million and the new Touchstone Studio of Walt Disney was smelling sweet. As was the career of one Tom Hanks, who didn't forget what director Ron Howard had done for him.

"He has seen absolutely everything that can possibly happen on a set," said Tom. "The man started doing it three months before he was born or something like that.

"Seriously, Ronnie made me a movie star. That's what he did. A twenty-minute conversation with him made me realize what was at stake here and what was needed from me. It was the product of everything I had done up to that point, and it still wasn't going to be adequate for doing that role. Because that role was going to put demands on me as an actor that hadn't been put on me before. Ronnie literally grabbed me by the lapels and said, 'If you're going to come in here and be funny and throw off the wisecracks and go toe-to-toe with everybody else on the set, the movie will stink. No one's going to believe it and it'll be your fault.' Wow! He was right, too. I had to be Jimmy Stewart in *Splash*, goofy-looking but also relatively attractive, lovable, but mostly vulnerable, so when it comes down to you loving this woman, you have to love her. I'm just thankful he cleared that up at the start. He told me, 'You're not what the movie is about—Daryl is—but you're the catalyst for everything that goes on, and if we don't believe that you're really swept away by this woman . . . there's no movie here.' All this was laid out in front of me before the rehearsals even began."

The result was perhaps the quintessential Tom Hanks performance as the guy next door who gets the girl of his dreams. He is both goofy and dreamy, but utterly ingenuous and tender at the same time. As Allen Bauer, Tom Hanks combined his two sides—the two different personalities his good buddy Peter Scolari pointed out: the pie-in-the-sky dreamer/idealist and the nutty, glib Yuppie—to perfection and *Splash* ran with it from there.

Splash was filled with great moments, but perhaps no one scene captures the comic fantasy's true appeal more than the one in which Daryl Hannah chomps into her lobster, shell and all, in a fancy New York restaurant. As horrified patrons look on, Tom Hanks hides his own amazement with a loving, protective, yet exasperated expression that seems to say, "What's the matter? Haven't you ever seen a girl eat lobster before?" That grace under befuddlement is what makes Tom Hanks more than just another young actor. It makes him a star.

6 Sophomore Jinx: *Bachelor Party* Bingo

"*Bachelor Party* was a movie that knew no rules whatsoever, a rock'n'roll sex comedy. The point of it was to make people laugh—sometimes it did, and at other times it didn't at all. But that's all right. Because even within these confines, there still has to be something that you're going to look at, so you come up with things, even if they're not built into the script."

—Tom Hanks

While *Splash* was still in postproduction in late 1983, Hanks, unaware of how well that movie would be received, signed up immediately to star in *Bachelor Party*, a son-of-*Animal House* teen gross-out sex comedy written by Neal Israel and Pat Proft, the same team responsible for *Police Academy*. Like any young actor, Tom struck while the iron was hot and his career was blooming. After all, he now had a second child, a girl, born in 1981 to go along with his older son Colin.

With motion picture stardom beckoning, he and Samantha and the kids moved to a home in the San Fernando Valley, and Tom began filming *Bachelor Party*.

The movie had its genesis in 1982 when producer Bob Israel, Neal's brother, was given his own bachelor party at the Hollywood Holiday Inn. "The lid came off that night," he recalled, and when the fizz died down he and partner Ron Moler realized they'd just lived through a highly commercial movie idea. They secured financing through Twin Continental Films and the movie was picked up for distribution by 20th Century Fox. Compared to *Splash*, *Bachelor Party* was a decidedly non-prestige project, but the eager Tom Hanks, fresh from his own initial starring role, had no way of knowing that.

Director Neal Israel tackled the project with craftsmanlike zeal, even insisting on a two-week rehearsal period before shooting began; highly unusual—and a luxury—for a low-budget film like *Bachelor Party*.

"That had to do with my theater background," explained Israel, who once apprenticed under famed Broadway producer/director/playwright George Abbot. "Directing for me comes out of character, and I like to have

the actors interrelate as the characters without the script, using improvisation. But most
of the movie was written down by the time
we came to shoot it—even Tom Hanks's
monologue in the kitchen as he throws around
the meatballs."

The premise of the movie is pretty basic.
Hanks is Rick Gassko, described in the production notes as "a carefree bus driver-about-
town who decides to give up his freedom for
rich and beautiful Debbie Thompson, the
woman he loves [played by voluptuous Tawny
Kitaen]. But there are obstacles to the marriage—most notably Debbie's parents, who
view the prospect with unabashed horror, and
her boyfriend Cole [Robert Prescott], an enraged preppie who will stop at nothing to get
Debbie back."

The plot, or what there is of it, centers
around—you guessed it—the bachelor party
Rick's buddies give for him on the eve of his
wedding to Debbie. Among his pals are Jay
(Adrian Zmed, of *Grease 2* as well as TV's
T.J. Hooker and *Dance Fever*) and Rudy (comedian Barry Diamond), who want to give
their lifelong friend a going-away party he'll
never forget. There are the predictable com-
plications, as plans include procuring the ser-

vices of prostitutes for the party and keeping Debbie and her folks in the dark about the whole thing, to say nothing of an enraged Cole stalking Tom Hanks like Wile E. Coyote speeding after the Roadrunner.

"This picture says that fidelity counts, sooner or later down the line," explained Tom Hanks in the movie's production notes. "The suspense for Rick is 'Will he, or won't he' at his own bachelor party. Whether he does or not can be the basis for the success or failure of his eventual marriage."

In fact, the situation Tom Hanks found himself in as Rick Gassko was not too far from what his real life was like at the time. His wife Samantha now had two children to take care of, putting her own acting/producing career on hold just as Tom's was taking off. The temptations were there and something Tom told a magazine about his own parents began to ring true.

"Essentially, my dad could afford and wanted to have kids, and my mom couldn't," he told *Cosmopolitan* magazine, explaining why that was the reason he and his older brother and sister stayed with their father while their younger brother lived with their mother. "She could really only afford to have the baby at the time."

"I'm a traditional kind of guy," said Hanks as Rick Gassko in *Bachelor Party*, and those values are reaffirmed in that film when Hanks resists all his pals' entreatments for a final fling before matrimony. He clings tenaciously to that loyalty and faithfulness despite his character's scripted flakiness.

"I don't think there's ever been a love story like this one," said director Israel, typically overstating the case for the in-house publicity. "We deal very honestly with what goes on at a bachelor party, so any woman whose fiancé is going to be honored with one should definitely see this movie. I just hope that we don't ruin it for anyone."

As long as you don't expect a cocaine-snorting donkey at your shin-dig! The film was completed on locations in Los Angeles and in a $1,000-a-day Art Deco hotel suite built on a soundstage at Hollywood's Laird Studios, modeled after a similar suite at Los Angeles' Biltmore Hotel, where many of the lobby, restaurant, hallway, and parking lot scenes were shot. The climactic finale, which includes an admittedly hilarious sequence in a 3-D movie house, was definitely a triumph of second-unit filmmaking. A wide-ranging, wall-to-wall rock'n'roll soundtrack was produced by Danny Goldberg and released on I.R.S., including such pop artists as R.E.M., Jools Holland, The Alarm, Oingo Boingo, Wang Chung, The Police, and The Fleshtones.

When the film was released in June of 1984, only three months after *Splash*, it appeared to be just another of those endless *Porky's* teen sex comedies. Three years later, with all the rampant paranoia about AIDS, the film's drug and sex jokes seem rooted in another era altogether. Still, despite the movie's leering pretext—lots of sexist humor about heaving bosoms and carnal conquests—Tom Hanks emerges pretty much unscathed. In fact, his comedic instincts are allowed full reign (even with Neal Israel's insistence that most of the lines were written) because Hanks gives such a natural performance.

The audience likes Tom Hanks. He is a nice guy. Just as in his off-screen life, in *Bachelor Party* he is faced with the temptations of success—and he's begun to feel very guilty about it. Pegged as an attractive leading man, he tries, at home, to be a loving husband and father to his wife and two kids. Just as with

Rick Gassko in the movie, we root for Hanks to overcome the demons and come out on top. Which is just what happens on the screen . . . and off.

Riding on the coattails of the tremendous success of *Splash*, *Bachelor Party* turned out to be a sleeper at the box office . . . in spite of almost universally negative reviews that the film's leading man miraculously avoided.

Variety commented, "*Bachelor Party* is another case of adults giving the kids what they think they want. Picture is too contrived to capture the craziness it strains for and ultimately becomes offensive rather than funny. . . . " But, they also went on to add, " . . . main reason to see the pic is for Hanks's performance. Recalling a younger Bill Murray, Hanks is all over the place, practically spilling off the screen with an overabundance of energy."

Indeed, the first part of *Bachelor Party* is virtually a one-man *tour de force*, a showcase for Tom Hanks's ability to steal a scene. The movie opens up with him portraying the bus driver for St. Gabriel's Catholic School. As the door opens to reveal a stern-faced nun, Hanks wisecracks, "Sister, if you ever get lonely after vestments, my number's in the book," at once disarming her icy gaze. It's a fine line that Hanks walks between impudence, arrogance, obnoxiousness, and charm—but he rarely falls off.

As he pulls away, all hell breaks loose on the bus. The charming little kids begin to shoot craps in the aisles. "Now don't forget, Garcia, ten percent goes to the house," says Hanks blithely.

Another classic Hanks scene is the one referred to by Israel as having been entirely scripted, the one where Rick cooks dinner. Tom floats around the kitchen, musing about how "dead animal's flesh is America's favorite meal," heating it up with a blow torch and, finally, serving a "chunky" potato salad that is nothing but whole potatoes sitting on a bed of lettuce. The other great Hanks moment occurs when he goes to dinner at his fiancée's stuffy parents' house and slams a tennis ball over the fence, screaming, "Cleveland wins the pennant!! Cleveland wins the pennant!!" At the dinner table, when informed there is no dog, he cracks, "What a waste of good fat!" while holding a plateful of leftovers. As his prospective father-in-law gets angrier, he pops out with, "We're adopting a seventeen-

Looking debonair and delightful.

© Phototeque

What a drag . . . Hanks and Peter Scolari in a scene from "Bosom Buddies."

Hanks and Peter Scolari.

© Ralph Dominguez/Globe Photos

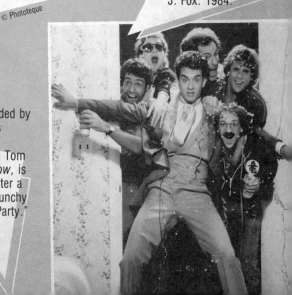

Tom Hanks, *above*, in a scene from "Family Ties" with Michael J. Fox. 1984.

© Phototeque

Surrounded by his raucous buddies, bridegroom Tom Hanks, *below*, is about to enter a rousing, raunchy "Bachelor Party."

How many men would gladly have swapped places for this scene? A first kiss with mermaid Daryl Hannah in "Splash."

© Phototeque

With a warm-blooded mermaid.

. . . on a bicycle made for three. Tom Hanks with Lori Singer and Jim Belushi, co-stars of the movie "The Man With One Red Shoe."

© Globe Photos

© Phototeque

Action anyone? Tom Hanks as Lawrence Bourne III in the comedy "Volunteers" with co-star John Candy.

© Phototeque

H anks is trying to restore his house and his relationship with Anna when her ex-husband played by Alexander Godunov pays a surprise visit in the movie, "The Money Pit."

F ilming the movie "The Money Pit" in New York City. 1985.

© Vinnie Zuffante/Star File

As advertising executive David Basner in "Nothing in Common."

Phototeque

Tom Hanks at a press conference in Los Angeles, September 1986.

© Frank Edwards, Fotos International

With his friend, actress Rita Wilson, at the Los Angeles premiere of "Nothing in Common." July 1986.

© Frank Edwards, Fotos International

© Charles Wenzelberg/Star File

Filming a scene from his new movie "Punchline" in New York. Hanks and co-star Sally Field have been rehearsing stand-up comedy to practice for their roles as comics.

year-old Korean girl I've had my eye on for some time, but don't worry, Dad, you'll have American grandchildren in no time." Upon leaving, he says goodbye to Mom, "Let's do this every day, Mrs. T.; I'll bring the wienies." When the nasty former boyfriend tries to bribe him with a cash offer not to marry, he replies, "What's Debbie's Blue Book value?"

Thanks to Hanks, *Bachelor Party* proved to be the actor's second most successful box office film (after *Splash*) to date, earning $19 million in theatrical rentals and over $35 million in gross revenue, according to *Variety*'s latest count. Considering the film cost less than $5 million to make, had no stars, and very little in the way of good critical notices, the success of *Bachelor Party* was credited to Tom Hanks and Tom Hanks alone. The movie didn't do wonders for the careers of Adrian Zmed, Tawny Kitaen, or Barry Diamond, did it? The picture also did incredibly well in its home video and subsequent cable incarnations.

"When I read the script, I thought it was a formula film, a rock'n'roll sex comedy essentially, and I wondered what the challenge was going to be," Tom told *Aquarian Weekly* in 1984. "How was this going to be interesting as opposed to cashing in on the craze? Being *Surf II* or *Porky's IX*. Well, the creative people actually wanted to get as far away from that as possible.

"Okay, fine, so this time, it was my turn to say, 'Let's turn on the creative juices and see what happens. Let's see what makes this cook.' At the same time I wasn't interested in throwing myself at a wall or dropping my pants. We needed to get something better."

What he got was something halfway between.

"What we did was to try to examine the idea of the bachelor party," he explained to the *Los Angeles Herald Examiner* at the time of the movie's release. "Is it a privilege? Is it a birthright? Is it an American tradition? Is it worthwhile at all? To have this one evening in a man's life be given over to total Dionysian revel. Or does fidelity count, sooner or later? The given is, will they both survive his bachelor party?"

At least Tom Hanks did, with career intact and flourishing. In fact, with two leading-man roles aided by two beautiful women (Daryl Hannah and Tawny Kitaen), Tom was fast becoming a very desirable sex symbol. He appeared in *Playboy* magazine, dispensing fashion advice.

"When it comes to clothes, I don't get real carried away. I don't particularly like getting dressed up, though sometimes I have to— for meetings or talk-show appearances. That's when the wardrobe department comes in handy. What I do is use the clothes I've kept from movie or TV roles. They're one of the better perks.

"What I really like, though, are jive clothes. Levi's 501s, for example, are the best. I wear them all the time. The fit and the ease and the comfort—you just can't beat it. And with them, I'll wear T-shirts or cotton long-sleeved shirts. They have to be cotton, though—no synthetics. My real favorites now are Japanese baseball jerseys. They're not easy to find, but they're well worth the trouble.

"I used to love wearing plaid-flannel shirts, but I can't anymore. Every homosexual in New York started to wear them, and it got to be too much. I had to stop. Some people thought I was strange enough as it was after what I wore on *Bosom Buddies*."

Despite his rapid rise to stardom, Tom tried

to maintain a normal home life. He stead-
fastly refused to talk about his wife or children in the press, wondering aloud how it
would affect Samantha's career to be referred to as Mrs. Tom Hanks.

"I'm your average family Joe," he told *Teen*
magazine, echoing his line in *Bachelor Party*
about being a traditional kind of guy. "When
I'm not working, I like the routine of getting
up in the morning, taking care of the house
and the kids, then sitting down and having
some coffee. Then I just like to piddle around.
I talk on the phone, watch television, read,
and that's about it. I like boredom—I save
the exciting stuff for work."

But Tom wouldn't have that luxury too much
longer. From *Bachelor Party*, he went straight
on location to *The Man with One Red Shoe*,
shot in Washington, D.C. It was a remake of
the French farce, *The Tall Blonde Man with
One Black Shoe*, and produced by Victor Drai
and directed by Stan Dragoti. And, after that,
Volunteers.

While there was a lot of goodwill toward
Tom Hanks at this point, both from an audience and critical standpoint, the actor himself realized how easily that type of senti-

ment could turn. In fact, his character in *Bachelor Party*, unlike the heroic Allen Bauer of *Splash*, even showed signs that quick wit could be misinterpreted.

"I've been slammed. I've been called half-baked. My flipness comes off as a smartass quality that a lot of people don't like," he complained to a reporter. "It's a high-pressure business."

As for his burgeoning popularity as a glamorous movie star, he was typically self-effacing, "I don't think I'm ugly, but I do sometimes look in the mirror and say, 'What is with these lips?'"

When prodded about doing a lowbrow film like *Bachelor Party*, he didn't feel the need to apologize. "This is what I do," he insisted to *Rolling Stone*. "I'm an actor. An actor has to act. What else am I supposed to do—sit around the house?"

Coming off two big hits his first two times out, that wasn't very likely. . . .

"Yes, doing *Bachelor Party* is not like doing *Richard III* or *Henry IV, Part II*, but that doesn't diminish the joy of scoring off something that somebody else has written. In fact, at times, it can be more difficult, just walking down a hall and talking to somebody and making that interesting. That's what I find to be the biggest challenge in making movies.

"Doing Shakespeare and *Bachelor Party* is not that different, actually. The cerebral processes are the same. The demands are certainly different. The overall appreciation is going to be different. Doing Shakespeare, doing classical theater is a luxury."

A luxury that Tom Hanks could no longer afford.

7　Fiddling Around: *The Man with One Red Shoe*

The Man with One Red Shoe was an American remake of the popular French film, *The Tall Blonde Man with One Black Shoe,* one of those lightweight farces of mixed identities the French seem to be able to churn out effortlessly. The 1972 original was directed by Yves Robert and starred Pierre Richard in the title role. Producer of the new version, Victor Drai, who had previously adapted Robert's *Pardon Mon Affaire* as *The Woman in Red* for Gene Wilder, had originally sought an older, more established actor for the role of Richard Drew, the young violinist who becomes an inadvertent pawn in a power game between rival factions of the C.I.A. *The Tall Blonde Man* was just one of several French films to which Drai acquired the rights when he formed his production company in 1983 (after pursuing successful careers in French fashion and California real estate).

He explained that was the fastest way to get started in the movie business. "Studio production deals are most easily made with presold properties like bestsellers," he said. "But these are hard to acquire if you are a newcomer with no track record."

Since he was familiar with the repertoire of French cinema, Drai had access to many of the films and, equally important, as an eight-year Hollywood resident, he understood the tastes and demands of an American audience.

"I think a great story can be adapted to any country," he said at the time. "And this particular film had a great basic story: When an innocent man is put under surveillance, everything he does suddenly looks suspicious."

Drai immediately offered the film to director Stan Dragoti, whose work included the box office successes *Love at First Bite* and *Mr. Mom*, but whose career had stalled due to a cocaine bust while traveling in Berlin. He took the assignment and reached an agreement with his old buddy Drai before a deal was even finalized with a studio.

A lifelong movie buff and award-winning commercial director (he did the famous "I Love New York" spots), Dragoti had showed a flair for comedy in his previous work.

"The picture makes a statement," he said. "Caught in a crazy, totally immoral conflict, two men act morally and are rewarded—one with love, one with success. Of course, my primary concern was to keep the audience on the edge of their seats even while they are laughing, and this screenplay had that potential. This is a classical cause-effect story in which everything builds logically from the initial premise. You don't see much of that anymore: first act, second act, third act. What you get today is mostly 'and-then' writing: This happened and then that happened and then something else, with no causal link connecting them."

The time-span of *The Man with One Red Shoe* is less than two days of nonstop action, from the moment Tom Hanks steps off the plane wearing one red sneaker to the ending when the entire mess is cleared up. As mentioned before, Hanks was not the first choice to play the role of Richard Drew. Ultimately, he was selected because, as Drai saw it, "he was refreshing and new." As Hanks was a classically trained stage actor with a flair for light comedy, Drai felt this role drew equally on the performer's talents as a romantic lead as well as a deft slapstick comedian. Once again, he gets the girl, in this case, the lovely Lori Singer, who'd launched her career in the television series *Fame* (like Hanks did with *Bosom Buddies*) and then went on to star in *Footloose, The Falcon and the Snowman*, and *Trouble in Mind*. As the double agent assigned to Hanks—she eventually falls in love with him, of course—Lori makes another perfect mate for our hero.

"Lori is a sweet and marvelous girl," said Tom. "Very sure of what she wanted to do, and sometimes downright adamant about what she felt her character should be doing. You have to be impressed with someone who approaches a role from the very beginning with such conviction."

As for director Stan Dragoti, Hanks claimed,

"When I sat down with him three months before I went into the movie, I was still kicking around whether I wanted to even go about doing a remake, especially something that was so affectionately remembered as *The Tall Blonde Man with One Black Shoe*, a movie that can really only be done by the French because that's the way they view the world.

"Our movie was incredibly constructed, the kind of thing where one person is observing me in a room and there are other people observing him observing me . . . it's like boxes within boxes within boxes. It was almost like a battle to clear the head away from doing anything that is going to take away from the main thrust of that big beat. It was very tough and almost confining—it was an opportunity for me to get juice out of the refrigerator. This is literally what I had to do . . . I had to discover ways of doing that which wouldn't be pedestrian. That is the most nitpicking, nickel-and-dime stuff about making a movie, the hardest to really comprehend."

Hanks plays Richard Drew, a concert violinist totally wrapped up in music. He inadvertently becomes the pawn of a plot hatched by a pair of rival C.I.A. factions headed up by character actors Charles Durning and

Dabney Coleman. Hanks is set up, quite by chance, as a fake agent, and immediately becomes the target of intensive surveillance by both sides. Lori Singer becomes involved as an agent assigned to force him to spill the beans, and the film derives its comedy from the oblivious Hanks as the innocent bystander walking through a gauntlet of intelligence agents. As the plot thickens, the hapless Drew is hit with a poison dart, has his apartment ransacked, and is seduced by a beautiful double agent while being observed through a two-way mirror. Costars include Jim Belushi as Hanks's musician buddy and Carrie Fischer as Belushi's horny wife.

Shooting began on the movie in Washington, D.C. in August, 1984, with two separate units filming simultaneously and coordinating the shuttling of personnel and equipment through the production office. Meanwhile, back in Hollywood at the Fox studios, interior sets were being designed and built on five different soundstages, with more than a half-million dollars worth of state-of-the-art electronic equipment used on one set alone. The outer office of the tour bus company that served as the front for a spy operation was constructed in a vacant building within sight of Capitol Hill, while its back room was being built 3,000 miles away on Stage 15 on the 20th Century lot.

While the high-tech world of the C.I.A. was visually dramatic, Tom Hanks's apartment received more thought and care than any of the other sets. Thorough in his preparation, Hanks, along with production designer Dean Mitzner, visited the apartments of several musicians in the Georgetown section of Washington to check out how they really lived. Once the apartment's design had been determined, the set decorator went to work rounding up the appropriate furnishings, highlighted by a collection of antique musical instruments that included two rare eighteenth century serpent *forveilles* (forerunners of the tuba), a *biwa* (Japanese moon guitar), a *mando dello*, and a solid ivory side-blown bass horn made from an elephant tusk in Kenya more than 150 years ago, according to the film's production notes.

Filming completed in Washington at the end of August and returned to Los Angeles after Labor Day for four weeks of local locations, among them the new Bradley Terminal at Los Angeles International Airport (sitting in for Dulles) and the inside of Los

Angeles City Hall (subbing for the Senate).
The interior of Kennedy Center was repro-
duced on soundstage 6 and provided the scene
of three major musical debuts—Jim Belushi
on tympani, Carrie Fisher on flute, and Tom
Hanks playing "Scheherezade" on the violin.

He learned to play the instrument just for
the part in three months.

"Although I'd played the violin for a couple
of years in elementary school, all I really knew
was how to hold the bow. In the movie, I
have to play the solo from 'Scheherezade'
with the symphony and also the love song I
write to Lori Singer, and we were determined
that it would look authentic on the screen."

Fox music consultant Richard Kaufman, who
lived around the corner from Hanks, began
to teach the actor the instrument on July 4th,
which initiated a regimen for Tom of walking
to his tutor's house daily and practicing for
two hours. When he played with the orchestra on screen, you can see his bow and fin-
gers moving in unison, though the music was
overdubbed.

"The pressure was intriguing, but it gave
you the most incredible creative buzz," he
recalled.

In addition, Hanks did a great deal of research for his role as concertmaster of the fictitious Washington Symphony, attending several rehearsals of the Los Angeles Philharmonic and replacing the rock'n'roll on his car stereo with classical music. He also talked to several classical musicians and visited them in their homes to further hone his characterization of Richard Drew.

"They were bright, stimulating people," he said, "eclectic in their interests and varied in their personalities. But they were all bad dressers, which they blamed on lack of money. You can see that reflected in my wardrobe on screen."

And goes a long way toward explaining why it is that Tom Hanks is wearing one red sneaker, the title change of which was his idea, too.

"I pointed out since I was neither tall nor blond, the original film title wouldn't work," admitted Hanks, who added that a member of the crew suggested "one red shoe" for color when *The Man with One Black Shoe* sounded a little flat.

Unfortunately, with all the work and care put into the film, along with its talented cast and crew, *The Man with One Red Shoe* was soundly lambasted by the critics when it opened on July 19, 1985, the first of two Hanks films which would open within a single week of one another. Not even Tom Hanks avoided the negative notices this time around.

The *New York Times* said, "Victor Drai . . . appears to be making a career out of demonstrating how poorly French farce can travel . . . *The Man with One Red Shoe* loses a lot in translation . . . it's mostly just slight, and none of it elicits more than the mildest of chuckles. The leading role, played in blank rather than deadpan style by Tom Hanks, is a more neutral presence than Mr. Richard, who seemed to move through his version of the story in a state of blissful obliviousness. The real trouble, though, is that what was once an airy comedy of errors has been staged in a more literal sitcom style, which makes the story's silly turns of circumstance look absurd."

Variety chimed in, "Except for stretches of rather amusing pointlessness, *The Man with One Red Shoe* doesn't look to be much of a summer comedy entry. No matter the color, the shoe has no box office leg to fit . . . Hanks is okay at his ill-defined duties, but . . . never funny enough to overcome the damage to his likability."

USA Today didn't care much for the movie, but did have some kind words for its star: "Tom Hanks, thankfully scrapping his *Bachelor Party* loutishness for some of his old *Splash* charm, is rather endearing as the classical musician who is arbitrarily caught in a power play . . . he seems refined enough to play in an orchestra, yet klutzy enough to get the hair of a beautiful blond spy [Lori Singer] caught in his zipper."

When he originally took the role, Tom Hanks undoubtedly saw the movie as one of those classic Alfred Hitchcock innocent-man-caught-in-a-web-of-intrigue type of movies, the kind Cary Grant used to pull off so effortlessly. Certainly the concept of a regular guy suddenly being thrust into the middle of a Spy *vs.* Spy situation had all the earmarks of the sort of role Tom Hanks played best.

"It was never a question of what was funnier or would get the most laughs, but of making it as interesting as possible," he said of the role. "The guy is totally reactive, and Stan and I agreed that playing it for klutziness was too limiting—a one-joke thing. The character as we developed him tends to be myopic because of his passion for music, but he has many other interests as well, and he's not an incompetent when the girl he loves is threatened."

Nevertheless, the movie's most effective moments are precisely when Hanks is doing physical comedy, as when he falls to the ground after being hit by the poison darts, or when he gets poor Lori's hair stuck in his zipper. Unfortunately, there is never any human side to the film's mechanics, a problem that would plague Hanks once again in *The Money Pit*. The audience likes to see Tom Hanks as a regular guy, but he also must show some true personality, something he never really gets a chance to do in the tightly constructed mechanistic world of the big-budget *Red Shoe*.

Not surprisingly, the film was Tom Hanks's first failure, artistically and commercially. The movie absolutely died at the box office, one of Fox's big-budget disasters of the year, earning less than $4.3 million in rentals and a gross of slightly over $8 million. Still, Tom Hanks insisted he had nothing to apologize for.

"Listen, I loved my character in the movie," he told the *Los Angeles Times*. "I thought it was great, that he was totally oblivious to all the craziness around him. Yet the movie went down the tubes.

"I think sometimes you put all this work into a film, but the actual theme—the thing that makes people out there really *care* about the movie—gets lost along the way."

After completing the filming of *The Man with One Red Shoe* on November 8, 1984, Hanks didn't have time to sit and contemplate; he was immediately off to the outskirts of Otatitlan in southern Mexico for an entirely different role, that of the upper class Lawrence Bourne III in Nicholas Meyer's comedy about the Peace Corps, *Volunteers.* In it, Tom would be reunited with his *Splash* sidekick, John Candy. Hanks's two roles of 1984 couldn't be further apart, from the innocent nerd of *The Man with One Red Shoe* to the smooth-talking and cynical con artist of *Volunteers.* That difference was not lost on an eager Tom Hanks. Even though the C.I.A. is the bad guy in both films, Hanks's characters are quite distinct.

"While the roles I play are more or less a play on my persona, they always show different aspects of it," he explained. "Especially these two, back to back, they're almost opposite ends of the spectrum. Not just in terms of who the characters are and what they go through, but in terms of the nature of the comedy itself.

"A movie which is labelled a 'comedy' essentially means to the audience to come and see it and laugh . . . there's a fine bottom line, a very jagged edge, which you can really get hurt on if you're on the side of it which doesn't make people laugh.

"People come out of a comedy and may not like it. If you ask them why not, they'll say, it didn't make them laugh. End of critique. There's nothing else to say. And, if they did like it, that's also the end of the critique. It did its job. Within those parameters, there's always a huge jeopardy involved for everybody concerned, down to the prop guys and the set dressers. They have to look at something and think, 'This looks pretty, but is it funny? Does it add to the comedy?' So, everybody runs around with this horrible glazed look in their eyes, wondering if the movie is funny. . . . "

Director Stan Dragoti thought Hanks gave him just what he was looking for in *Red Shoe:* "Tom's greatest strength is that all audiences can relate to him. He's not staggeringly handsome, but he's so appealing and hip and interesting that you always care about what he's doing on the screen.

"He's also the consummate actor. In *Red Shoe*, he approached each scene fearlessly. For instance, at one point, his character is shot with tranquilizer darts. I asked him if he wanted me to hire some mimes who could show him how to react to being tranquilized, but Tom told me not to waste my money. And the scene worked perfectly."

Unfortunately for Tom Hanks and everyone else involved, *The Man with One Red Shoe*, as elaborate and carefully put-together as it was, didn't generate the necessary guffaws. It was a dud, pure and simple. At least, however, Tom Hanks had learned how to play the violin, although even he admitted that wasn't entirely necessary for movie authenticity. So much for method acting.

"It was a mistake," Hanks admitted ruefully to *New York* magazine about the music lessons. "I should have learned to act playing the violin. I thought I botched it."

As for the movie itself, Hanks wasn't too concerned. "I wasn't shocked it failed. I saw the original and felt about the same as I do about our movie. It's not *Star Wars*."

8 Down Mexico Way: Hanks Finds Love in *Volunteers*

"I'm twenty-eight, and growing up in the seventies was pretty weird. We 'Me Generation' people never had any ideals to sink our teeth into. That's why I'm so good at playing people who are, more than anything else, confused."

—Tom Hanks in *Rolling Stone*

Tom Hanks is one of those 'tweeners, which means he's both too young to have been affected by the counterculture that influenced the likes of Warren Beatty, Robert DeNiro, William Hurt, Dustin Hoffman, and Al Pacino, yet too old for the materialistic Brat Pack antics of such actors as Matthew Broderick, Sean Penn, Judd Nelson, Emilio Estevez, Andrew McCarthy, and Jon Cryer. At thirty-one years of age, there are still some pangs for those lost days of peace and love. In one particular

Bosom Buddies episode, Hanks flashed back to his high school days as a drug-addled hippie. Throughout his film appearances there have been frequent rock'n'roll references and popular culture allusions. On the other hand, starting from *Bosom Buddies'* Kip, Hanks has frequently played the quintessential Yuppie, from the love-crazed Allen Bauer in *Splash* to befuddled fiddler Richard Drew in *Red Shoe* to rock lawyer Walter Fielding in *The Money Pit* and ad whiz David Basner in *Nothing in Common.* All very glib, unabashedly ambitious, and materialistic young urbane professionals. Yet these characteristics have been coupled with a charming ability to puncture the pretensions of the whole quest, which is Tom Hanks's saving grace. He can be smart-alecky and obnoxious, but he's cute, too—so he's forgiven.

This quicksilver ability to shift between straight and hip culture is at the root of Hanks's appeal. It is the core of what Huey Lewis came to call "hip to be square": a combination of absolute cockiness and witty self-effacement which translates well on the screen.

In Nicholas Meyer's *Volunteers,* Tom Hanks confronts the duality of his character: the wise-guy and the saint. Hanks first read the script for this comedy about the U.S. Peace Corps building a bridge in Thailand back in 1981.

"I wanted to do it right then, but I wouldn't have been ready to," he told *Family Weekly.* "The stuff I've been able to do in this has been culled from all the work I've done up to this point because this is the most constantly demanding role I've ever had. The concentration and disciplinary factors I've been notoriously lacking in my entire career up to this point are now necessary. This is the first job I've had where the gut instinct was not all that was necessary. I've had a lot of jobs, especially in TV, where that was all you had to work on because you don't have the time to explore anything else. But, on this movie, I saw a dialogue coach; there were aspects of fashion and dress I had to get down. When it comes to fashion, I'm basically a lox. I don't care what I wear . . . but . . . the events and the characters just mesh real well. It's all in the script. Without being locked into the perceptions of 1962, I think we ended up taking all the images of that era and adding to it the social consciousness we've gained since then.

"I mean the naivete of what these people are attempting to do is almost embarrassing . . . the idea that young earnest Ameri-

cans can just go and make everything wonderful because we have this enthusiasm and
we're the best and the brightest. We'll just
sweep in there, and, as the John Candy character puts it, 'We'll have this place running
like Pittsburgh in three weeks.' Now, why in
the hell would you want this place to be running like Pittsburgh? That's what makes my
character almost vomit with nausea, but then
he turns around and sees reason to go ahead
and pursue this."

It's not hard to see what attracted Tom
Hanks to the screenplay of *Volunteers*. His
role, that of the spoiled Yalie Lawrence Bourne
III, requires Hanks to adopt a snooty Brahmin
New England accent which is one-third JFK,
one-third Cary Grant, and one-third William
F. Buckley. For the first time, Hanks is playing
a discernible character, and a vaguely smug
and unlikable chap at that, although Tom still
fills him with endearing qualities.

The film takes place in 1962, with Bourne
graduating from college. Turns out the play-
boy/*bon vivant* has run up a huge gambling
debt, swollen by a graduation-day loss in-
curred when the Lakers lose to the Celtics
110–107 in the NBA finals. This requires Larry
to hightail it to the airport, where he switches

places with his college roomie as the latter is about to board a jet to Thailand to serve a term in the Peace Corps. Bourne gets aboard only to run into gung-ho superpatriot John Candy as "Tom Tuttle from Tacoma" and a planeload of do-gooders chanting "Michael Row Your Boat Ashore" and "Puff the Magic Dragon." A slightly hungover, extremely cynical Lawrence Bourne III has a look that says he's died and gone straight to hell without passing Go.

The movie intends to be a spoof of early sixties idealism and altruism, what JFK meant when he said, "Ask not what your country can do for you, but what you can do for your country." It was still the era of Kennedy's Camelot and youthful presidency, and into this environment comes Tom Hanks's wise-cracking Yuppie-of-the-eighties transposed back into a spoiled-playboy-of-the-sixties, sporting a white dinner jacket that is so out of place only Hanks himself could pull it off.

Volunteers grew out of an idea from two Stanford University graduates, producer Walter Parkes and writer Keith Critchlow, who thrashed out the story while en route to the very last Tehran Film Festival a few months before the fall of the Shah. At some point on the seventeen-hour flight, reminiscent of the one Lawrence Bourne takes in *Volunteers*, the film began to take shape.

"We thought it would be interesting to take the *least* likely Peace Corps candidate, somebody totally devoid of any altruism, and plunk him down in the middle of the jungle," said Parkes. Part of the story's appeal came from the character of Bourne, the upper class twit who ends up in Thailand. "After a couple of decades of angst-ridden heroes, Lawrence is kind of wonderfully unneurotic. Compared to almost everybody he meets, his motives are crystal clear—he's out to have a good time and he doesn't care who knows it.

"But at the same time, he's kind of a Rick Blaine character. He starts out as a guy who, like Bogart said in *Casablanca*, sticks his neck out for nobody. By the end of the film, he's risking that neck for the sake of a village he's grown to love."

Five years elapsed between that germ of a notion and the film's release in the summer of 1985. Photography for the film began on November 23, 1984 in southern Mexico, in the jungle outside Chiltepec, Oaxaca, and in

Churusbusco Studios, which had been previously refurbished to shoot *Dune* and the
two *Conan* films by Dino De Laurentiis.

In the half-forgotten Mexican town of Tux-
tepec, Oaxaca, a torturous three-hour drive
from Vera Cruz, Nicholas Meyer, a novelist
turned director who helmed the sci-fi comedy
Time After Time, as well as *Star Trek II* and
the much-heralded TV movie, *The Day After,*
set up camp for *Volunteers,* written by the
team responsible for TV's M*A*S*H, Ken Levine and David Isaacs.

"I read the screenplay when I was on my
honeymoon," he told *Film Comment.* "I
couldn't stop laughing. But what appealed to
me the most was its extreme literacy. It's
somewhat reminiscent of *A Midsummer
Night's Dream,* in the same way that *Bringing
up Baby* was its cinematic equivalent. There
is plenty of blue-collar movie-making these
days, with everybody saying, 'Fuck you.' I
prefer to see—and make—movies of a different kind."

Despite the potential hazards of the film
sites, coproducer Richard Shepherd said, "It
was one of the happiest shoots I can remember. Despite just about every conceivable
natural problem: coral snakes, for instance,

and rain, general bad weather, bugs. And mud. Lots of mud. But even with all those things, it was a very relaxed, happy crew. And I think a lot of that is due to Tom and John, who were just great to get along with, no star attitudes or anything."

"On a certain level," Meyer said, "the odds on this movie could be computed on a rather depressing configuration: Mexico for Thailand, a mixed Thai-Mexican crew, three or four languages on the set . . . but it's the easiest movie I've ever shot and certainly the most fun. All my nightmares about not getting the extras to understand me proved wrong. I didn't see dailies; they were put on cassettes and sometimes they arrived and sometimes they didn't."

Produced by HBO as part of their limited partnership, Silver Screen, and distributed by the newly formed Tri-Star (a joint company owned by HBO, Columbia, and Coca Cola), *Volunteers* was not a cheap movie to make. Expectations were high that the Hanks–Candy comedy pairing would duplicate the success of *Splash.*

Volunteers opened one week after *The Man with One Red Shoe*, on July 26, 1985. The film's reviews were fairly mixed, though there

were nice writeups in the *New York Times,
Time,* and *Newsweek.*

The *Times* said, "Take a healthy helping
of *Raiders of the Lost Ark,* a dollop of *The
Bridge on the River Kwai,* a dash of any Tar-
zan movie, a soupçon of *Casablanca,* a whiff
of *The Wizard of Oz,* and a stunt or two from
a favorite Saturday serial, stir frenetically,
and, if you're lucky enough to have snappy
dialogue by Ken Levine and David Isaacs, you
may end up with as funny a movie as *Volunteers.* . . ."

The reviewer called Tom Hanks's performance "stylishly droll. He is a center of confidence among the frantic goings-on, turning
peril into opportunity with an accent and
aplomb that are the birthright of an eighth-
generation Bourne."

Newsweek wrote: "It's Hanks, however,
who gives the movie its seductively sardonic
spirit. His character requires both the outsider smirk of a Bill Murray and the debonair
inside moves of a Cary Grant, and Hanks has
both. His brainy self-interest cuts through the
cant."

Time said, "Hanks has devised a snooty
accent (he sounds as if he were born with a
silver potato in his mouth) and a way of lik-

ably parodying almost Ayn Randian selfishness."

Hanks himself took pointers on portraying Bourne by studying his costar George Plimpton. "I tried to cull from him that air, not of superiority, but of a kind of confidence," Tom told the *Times.* "It was the most fun I've ever had as an actor. As soon as I put on that double-breasted white tuxedo, I was in character. It was a situation of the clothes making the man."

According to Hanks, Lawrence is "a guy who refused to take life on anything but its own terms. He is consistent to the end."

Something he shared with his creator.

Despite the critical raves, *Volunteers* was only slightly more successful than the disastrous *The Man with One Red Shoe,* earning a little more than twice that film's puny grosses, with theatrical rentals of $8.9 million and grosses of approximately $16 million. The movie was widely regarded as a box office flop, Hanks's second in one season.

Volunteers is a schizophrenic film. The opening scenes, with a dapper Hanks winning an outrageous card game from a gang of rough-looking dudes, then losing his double-or-nothing bet on a basketball game, (which he respectfully listens to at commencement, with earphones) make for a promising beginning. Likewise, the introduction of Candy as the mad do-gooder "Tommy Tuttle from Tacoma," whose favorite book is *Maximizing Growth Potentialwise*, is amusing. As is the sight of Tom Hanks in a white tuxedo landing in Thailand amid a bunch of starving peasants, only to explain to a Peace Corps representative, "It's not that I can't help these people. I just don't want to." Certainly that line was a great 1980s piss-take on 1960s idealism.

Unfortunately, the film devolves into some very, very broad slapstick, with Candy getting captured by the Communists and Tom Hanks courting his female costar, Rita Wilson, by trying to convince her he's not such a bad sort after all. In the final analysis, the Hanks character ends up saving the village from both the Communists and the drug dealers by deftly foiling their plans to take over a bridge being built by the blissfully unaware Peace Corps. Hanks ends up with the girl, and decides not to leave the land he's learned to love . . . and has learned to love him.

Of course, what's most fascinating now about *Volunteers* in the context of the Tom

Hanks story is his relationship with costar Rita Wilson, who plays Beth, an idealist first seen clutching a dog-eared copy of *Profiles in Courage* on the plane.

At the time, Tom praised her acting and recalled an appearance she had made on *Bosom Buddies*, where she played, ironically enough, Peter Scolari's girlfriend. In that episode, they met at a video dating service only to reveal that she was a worshipper of Satan, effectively scaring Scolari away.

"Rita's great. She was on an episode of *Bosom Buddies*, but I didn't have a scene with her. We just sat across the table from each other. For somebody who's making her first movie, she's amazingly cool, not cocky. She was making a good living doing commercials and TV, but she chucked it all to study in London for a year at the Academy of Music and Dramatic Art."

It might not have been love at first, or even second sight for Tom Hanks—after all, he was married at the time, with two children—but the man was obviously smitten, attracted to Rita's serious acting background and single-minded devotion to craft which, in many ways, mirrored his own. Ironically enough, it was on another Nicholas Meyer movie, *Time*

After Time, that actor Malcolm McDowell met *his* future wife, Mary Steenburgen. The guy must run the most loving sets in Hollywood.

It took a long time for Hanks to admit that he was in love with Wilson, but he finally spilled the beans to a persistent *Cosmopolitan* reporter. "I'd really rather . . . it's very difficult to get into. I don't want us to become some personality duo, but I'll say this much: I'm mad about the woman. I love her a lot. She's fabulous. We got to know each other over the course of four months. It was a slow dawning. There's something incredibly special about her."

Volunteers was Tom Hanks's biggest risk as an actor. Though the film found few takers, *Esquire* praised him as having given "a fully sustained comic performance." His director, Nicholas Meyer, gave him the ultimate compliment.

"Directing Tom Hanks is like driving a Maserati—you touch it and the whole thing roars off," he said.

The film's coproducer, Richard Shepherd, likened Hanks to Jack Lemmon in his ability to be wildly antic while at the same time maintaining credibility and sweetness.

"Tom has the internal integrity and vulnerability that would allow him to play a real wastrel and still get away with it."

"When I first met Nick, he slapped my face with a challenge right from the very beginning," said Hanks about his director. "Things like the dialect, which at that point I hadn't even considered. The New England accent adds a whole element to it and doesn't become a joke unto itself. Nick isn't exactly the most hilarious guy you're ever going to meet, but what he does have is a great affection for actors and a massive head. He can hold court better than anybody I've ever seen."

Hanks had a good time doing the part. He identified with the character's self-reliance and ability to relate to people, as well as his growing social conscience, despite the fact that he played a guy you wouldn't exactly admire at first. . . .

"I think I did my best work in developing this role because the guy was unlikable to a degree," Tom told *Cable Guide.* "I think he was the most dynamic character I ever played in that he was the most perfectly formed on paper. It was literally my job to take all of the necessary steps to fill him out—working on his voice and clothes, stuff like that."

One moment, Hanks is kibbitzing the villagers with some obscure variations on poker, only to reveal a more deeply spiritual side the next. Once again, Peter Scolari's statement about the two Tom Hanks seems awfully close to the mark.

"My character finally becomes involved, but in his own very particular way and for his own very particular reasons. This is a guy you hate to love. He's not a jerk or an idiot. He's very smart, cool but not calculating. When he comes up against an adversary, he'll convince them that they have no reason to hurt him. Or, as he says in the movie, 'You can't do this to me. I'm very rich and I have certain rights,'" said Hanks.

About the movie's crash at the box office, Tom was sanguine. "Remember, it was the great Rambo summer and I think philosophically, there are aspects of the movie that were not overly popular. It dealt with the Peace Corps during the idealistic sixties, and the subliminal theme of the movie was that just because we're Americans doesn't mean we have all the answers. That was a gung-ho period in which we thought we were the best and brightest, pure and simple. We had not only the wonders of technology that were developed through the American system, but we also had the freedom of thought that went along with the free enterprise system. But remember, Kennedy's Camelot only lasted nine hundred days or whatever it was, and I guess in the movie we were kind of hinting that although it didn't all die that November day, there was already some erosion of the ideal."

And, in the summer of 1985, fueled by Stallone's simplistic solutions, the American public didn't want to know they were less than omnipotent, especially in Southeast Asia. *Volunteers* probably fell victim to that belief as much as anything, but Tom Hanks still came out smelling like a rose. With a new part in a brand-new big-budget Steven Spielberg movie called *The Money Pit.* And a brand-new romance that was about to blossom and cause major changes in his domestic life.

9 Spielbergian Slapstick: Making *Money Pit*

"I've learned to accept personal failure without being completely demoralized by it for long periods of time. You can't let that bad dog follow you around for the rest of your life. And you can't believe the hype in either direction. Otherwise, it's peptic ulcer time and you start to beat the kids."

— Tom Hanks, *Moviegoer*, August 1985

A large part of Tom Hanks's charm and success as an actor comes from his ability to react quickly, turning what seems to be an imminent disaster into an advantage. Such technique has served him well on the screen, where his nimble characters use verbal dexterity to alleviate themselves from a potentially dangerous conflict. This has been a Tom Hanks trademark from his days sparring with costar Peter Scolari in *Bosom Buddies*; *Volunteers'* Lawrence Bourne III is perhaps the ultimate example of Hanks playing someone who gets by sheerly on the force of personality.

Hanks has also shown an uncanny ability to keep his career growing despite a series of out-and-out flops. (In fact, after the initial one-two punch of *Splash* and *Bachelor Party*, Hanks would strike out twice in a row with the disastrous summer 1985 doubleplay of *Volunteers* and *The Man with One Red Shoe*.) Still, the important thing for a young actor is work, and Tom Hanks was still a hot commodity in Hollywood. And, his next project, *The Money Pit*, sounded very promising. A big-budget comedy loosely based on *Mr. Blandings Builds His Dream House*, the film was to be produced by Steven Spielberg's Amblin Entertainment, headquartered at MCA's Universal Studios. Actor Richard Benjamin, who had helmed the comedy *My Favorite Year*, came aboard as the movie's director.

"I was attracted by the concept of physical comedy played alongside the story of a romantic relationship," Benjamin explained about the script, which was penned by veteran David Giler, whose writing credits included *The Parallax View* and *Fun with Dick and Jane*, as well as production credits on *48 Hours* and both *Aliens*. The director was also drawn to the idea of slapstick. "You see dialogue jokes and the like, but we have gig action gags that really happen—not faked optically or anything like that. I didn't think there was any other way to do it than have Tom Hanks perform many of his own stunts in the film. We made sure it was safe, of course, but it's fun to see him in the midst of things."

Once again, Hanks was cast opposite a beautiful leading lady (in this case, Shelley Long) as Walter Fielding, a lawyer for rock'n'roll groups. The *Cheers* star portrayed Anna Crowley, a classical musician who plays the viola and had been previously married to maestro Max Beissart, the egocentric orchestra conductor played by ballet star Alexander Godunov. The supporting cast included such standout performers as Maureen Stapleton, Joe Mantegna, Philip Bosco, Josh Mostel, Yakov Smirnoff, and Carmine Caridi.

Immediately after finishing *Volunteers*, and, obviously, months before its release, Hanks started filming *The Money Pit* in the spring of 1985. The film centers on Walter and Anna buying an old house and attempting to renovate while the place—and their relationship—deteriorates around them. The film had close to a $20 million budget, and, with the caliber of the talent assembled, Universal pinned its Christmas 1985 hopes on the Spielberg project, hoping to make the movie its big holiday release.

Hanks himself was hopeful. "It's all wonderful physical comedy, which starts very small, just a little broken step and then . . . we get into much more serious problems. I knew it was going to be a physical job, but when you first read the script, it only happens once. To shoot the sequence, though, you have to do it hundreds of times."

The scene he was referring to required the actor to be coated from head to foot in plaster for what seemed like days and days.

"There are pickmarks on my face from ashes and soot, from bricks and stones—while things hurl at me through pneumatic devices and blenders implode in my face, as do television sets.

"I look at it this way: There's an element of danger that you don't find in most professions. I like being the only member on the set who is not wearing a protective face-shield during the shot. And that's one of the reasons I was really anxious to take this job."

Once more, Hanks was attracted to the nitty-gritty, learning-on-the-run aspect of acting, the nuts and bolts, which had fascinated him since he was a young college student, nailing boards and carrying spears at the Great Lakes Shakespeare Festival. For Hanks, acting is an ongoing education, and he's tried to take a wide variety of roles to widen that learning process. For *The Money Pit*, he became a home expert.

"As soon as you have a stranger in your house with a tape measure on his belt, you're doomed, absolutely doomed," he joked about his character's dealing with contractors in the film. "You can't get off the operating table and say, 'Doc, you know, don't remove that tendon.' He'd say, 'Shut up, I'm a doctor, I know what I'm doing.' And that's what you have when you have anybody come to do anything at your house."

With the Steven Spielberg special-effects team in tow, the house in *The Money Pit* was turned into a living, breathing character itself; a Yuppie's worst nightmare come true—a home that's an absolute lemon.

"The house kind of said, 'Good morning' to you. Then it said, 'Get me some coffee, damn it,' and you went off and did it because it was *the* house," said Hanks.

Unfortunately for everyone involved, the house was practically the only thing that *was* alive in *The Money Pit*. Underneath all the ever-escalating, mechanized trappings, the movie had no real heart nor laughs, despite the best efforts of Hanks, Long, and Godunov to inject their romantic triangle with some emotion and humor.

The production was certainly physically impressive. Most of the interiors were filmed on the cavernous soundstage at the Kaufman Astoria Studios in Queens, N.Y. On the set, the house facade and interior rooms were painstakingly created, partially or completely demolished, and then later refurbished.

Other New York scenes were shot on Park Avenue, the roof of New York University, Soho, Central Park West, and the elegant Cafe Des Artistes near Lincoln Center.

Amadeus Oscar-winning Patrizia von Brandenstein designed the production, with months of planning going into the preparation of drawings and models, prior to set construction. Additional sequences were shot in Miami and on the Universal Studios lot. The major location was the Ridder (of the Knight-Ridder Syndicate) mansion on the North Shore of Long Island, which was already on the real estate block. During the course of the film, the house was demolished and rebuilt. No expenses were spared to make this film, but something was still left out.

"There's a line in the movie that is really wonderful because it has a double meaning for Shelley and I," explained Hanks. "The construction foreman says, 'Yeah, we thought we were gonna lose this house but the foundation is good, and if there's a good foundation you can withstand anything.' And that's what it's all about. Walter and Anna have a good foundation, and there's steel and backbone in a relationship like that."

Which was precisely what *The Money Pit* was lacking—human warmth—though, as always, Tom Hanks did the best with what he was given. In fact, he seemed to have more of a rapport with Shelley Long than he had with any of his previous costars. The two became close friends during the filming.

"We had miniature adventures, great philosophical discussions," said Hanks of his *Money Pit* mate. "We were playing two people who were very much in love, and that requires a certain kind of communication you're not going to invest in anybody else. I'm not saying I have to do this for the sake of the job, it just naturally happens. You end up finishing each other's sentences. It's not sexual, but it's intense, concentrated, packed, dense."

The Money Pit, though, turned into a white elephant of a movie, with the Rube Goldberg-type slapstick antics—as the house falls apart like a row of dominoes—taking precedence over any more personal interaction. When Universal took it off its Christmas 1985 schedule, the rumors began that the bloated production was in trouble. The film was finally released on March 26, 1986, to decidedly mixed notices. Most critics were turned off by the unrelenting focus on the crumbling house, saying it was too exaggerated—and too carefully plotted out—to even be funny.

The *New York Times* wrote, "If you can imagine a remake of Steven Spielberg's *Poltergeist* in which the spirits of the dead have been shoved aside by equally loud, unruly plumbers and carpenters, you'll have some idea of *The Money Pit*. . . . The comedy depends entirely on special electrical effects and outlandish physical gags, most of which have to do with heavy objects, including Walter, falling through floors, down staircases, and out windows . . . the film's approach to slapstick comedy recalls Mr. Spielberg's in the director's only outright failure—the monumental *1941*. The gags, though elaborately choreographed, are so clumsily broken up in bits and pieces of explanatory 'business' that one never has any sense of overall logic going fatally askew . . . the spectacle is so impressive, that you hesitate to laugh."

Newsweek wasn't much kinder, carping, "Instead of a real-estate fiasco anybody could roar at in recognition, *The Money Pit* has been inflated into a noisy destruction derby," though it did add, "the nimble Hanks again proves his delicious way with a doubletake."

USA Today said simply, "*Pit* is the pits . . . a dumb movie for grownups, but first-rate entertainment for kids."

Time was one of the few dissenters, praising "director Benjamin's gift for this kind of comic invention" and describing Tom Hanks as "poised between panic and exasperation with the kind of weird aplomb Cary Grant used to manage."

Despite the negative press, *The Money Pit* ended up with theatrical rentals of $16.2 million based on a $28 million gross, but with almost a $20 million budget, it was widely considered the first disappointment for Spielberg's Amblin Entertainment. Although it had second life as a top-selling videocassette, *The Money Pit* did not prove a showcase for Tom Hanks's talents as *Splash, Bachelor Party,* and even *Volunteers* had. Like *The Man with One Red Shoe, The Money Pit*'s pyrotechnics effectively shackled Tom Hanks in a web of special effects. As an acting exercise, the two films gave him a chance to show his slapstick prowess, but the actor's looks have never been what's endeared him to the public. It's his puppy-dog cuteness and regular-guy accessibility. Little wonder that Tom Hanks fans stayed away from *Red Shoe* and *Money Pit* for the most part. Still, with three sluggish box office performances in a row, Hanks maintained confidence in his abilities, even though he confessed to moments of doubt.

"I'll wake up at night," he told *Moviegoer*, "go into the bathroom, dab a little water on my face, look at myself in the mirror, and scream, 'What's happening to me? My career's all over!'

"But it would be the same thing if I were Ron of Ronco, the guy who invented the Pocket

Fisherman. Fear is an undeniable part of working in the movies, but it's a lot better than bouncing around on unemployment."

It's an attitude he's had since he performed Shakespeare to "two thousand completely uninterested public school students who just talked and threw stuff around the theater . . . I just busted my ass up there for two hours and they couldn't have cared less. But what can you do? I went out and had lunch," he explained.

"I've been in plays that stank to high heaven. But you've just got to shake it off. Most of the actors I know have had periods when they've been shit on, but you learn to take it and get on with life."

Tom Hanks persevered, and, before he was even finished with *The Money Pit*, he inked a development deal with Columbia Pictures that could potentially earn him upwards of $1 million per film, an incredible sum considering Tom had just five major motion pictures under his belt, only two of which had earned any substantial return at the box office.

"The best-case scenario is that I get to do stories and characters that are very interesting to me, and Columbia gets to make and

TOM HANKS • 153

distribute movies that make phenomenal amounts of money and go down in the annals of motion picture history," he deadpanned to *Cable Guide* about the pact. "The worse-case scenario is that everyone sits around and nothing gets done at all, and I go off into the apricot business or something like that. Somewhere in between there is where my deal falls."

The self-proclaimed "Average Joe" was one of Hollywood's most sought-after stars, though this didn't provide the expected solace in his personal life. In fact, the gap between Hanks and his wife Samantha was growing irrevocably at this point, despite the pair's joint production of Steve Tesich's *Passing Game* at Los Angeles's Gene Dynarski Theater in the spring of 1984. While Hanks's career had taken off, his wife's continued to stagnate, though Tom did everything he could to help, including producing *Passing Game* for her to star in.

"The reason I got involved was because of the impetus of my wife Samantha," he told *Drama-Logue*. "We had always been desirous to get into the producing aspect of theater, so this has been a learning-by-doing situation. We are already talking about two other projects we want to evolve. Sam is doing a supporting role in this and she swears she will never produce anything and be *in* it again. The pressures are just too great on both sides.

"Listen, it's been an experience for both of us," he continued. "I've been either driving a truck or pounding nails or sweeping up sawdust. I don't know if I can answer the question of *why* we are doing this. I don't know if I actually know. I think it goes back to a time when we were studying theater and we all thought it would be great if we could have our own space and do the plays we wanted to do with our own friends in them."

Actually, it would appear that Tom Hanks was trying to save his marriage. *Bosom Buddies* coproducer Ian Praiser told *Rolling Stone* that the young star wanted to maintain a normal existence.

"Tom wants to be just a guy. He battled success at first. It made him feel guilty."

Or as Tom himself added, "I don't view myself as particularly successful. I think of myself as lucky. I still work from the same set of insecurities as I always did. You know, do people really like me, and when will it all end?"

From all accounts, he is not that comfortable with his notoriety, and he has always tried to shield his family from the harsh glare of the media spotlight.

"There's an idea around that young actors are supposed to be mavericks," he told *Seventeen.* "Renegades running around doing God knows what when they're not working. You're never supposed to let on that you're married and have a family."

And yet his work was taking him away from them more and more . . . that coupled with a burgeoning romance with his *Volunteers* costar Rita Wilson.

"The job becomes your life," he said about his own work ethic. "The only yardstick for success is longevity."

And the key to longevity is more work. Which was why Tom Hanks immediately took on a movie being directed by Garry Marshall, whom he knew back from his TV days as the man behind such successful series as *Happy Days* and *Laverne and Shirley.* Once more, Hanks would play Mr. Yup, but this time he'd be required to stretch not just technically, but emotionally as well. With this film, he'd have to tap some of those long-suppressed feelings he had about his tumultuous upbringing . . . and come to terms with them.

Tom Hanks would be required to do something uncommon, and shift gears from laughs
to tears over the course of the movie. *Nothing
in Common* was to be Tom Hanks's rites of
passage as an actor . . . and it was the first
of his Columbia Pictures development deal,
making it an especially important film in more
ways than one.

"There definitely was a lot of familiar turf,"
he said to the *Los Angeles Times* about the
Nothing in Common script. "I guess you could
say I had a special frame of reference. It certainly raised the stakes a little."

Meanwhile, his own marriage was as shaky
as the house in *The Money Pit*.

10 An "Uncommon" Performance: Hanks Stretches Out

"Tom did what no one thought he could do. It's hard when you're coming from something like *Bachelor Party* to have someone say, 'Hey, kid! Cry!' But he did."
—Garry Marshall on Tom Hanks in *Rolling Stone*

"The verdict on Tom Hanks is that he's got it."
—Jackie Gleason in *Rolling Stone*

"You can only fall in love with a mermaid so many times . . . or sit on a scaffold and go, 'WAGAGAGAGA!'"
—Tom Hanks in *New York* magazine

After doing five comedies in a row, Tom Hanks approached the opportunity of playing *Nothing in Common*'s David Basner with relish ("and a hot dog . . . " as he might quip). Here was a role in which he could expand his range and not play second fiddle to female fish, dilapidated houses, high-tech gadgetry, rotund costars, or bikini-clad beauties.

"The timing for this movie was once in a lifetime," he told a syndicated radio reporter. "How often do you get a film that will demand everything that you know about yourself as an actor and as a human being? It's a grand palette of emotions . . . I worried whether we would be able to do it right. You take a huge risk in a movie like this, because you ask people to honestly laugh, but also to be honestly involved emotionally. This movie is as funny as everyday life is funny . . . and as involving as everyday life is involving. It walks that very fine line. I think the movie deals with a lot of gut-level emotions we can all relate to as members of the human race in 1986."

He refused to see the part as "getting serious." "To me, that's a ludicrous way of thinking," he explained to *Cable Guide*. "Because it implies that you weren't serious about the early stuff you did and that you didn't work hard on it, and now you're somehow working harder which in turn means you're more serious.

"*Nothing in Common* tries to show that life is funny and life is sad—all at the same time. We touch on a very common theme; that, deny it as much as we want to and run away from it as much as we want to, there is something in our blood that unites us with the people who gave birth to us. And there are times when we look at our parents and say we're not like them, we never will be, and we won't make the same mistakes—only to come to the shocking realization that we've all made the same mistakes our parents made and we're exactly like them."

It's a theme Hanks had stated before, but it never hit home with such force as it did in *Nothing in Common*.

"Some characters have nothing to do with you as a person; you create them from scratch," Hanks also said. "But occasionally, you have to draw from your own experience. That was the case here. I kept finding more of myself in this role, incorporating more of my life into this story. David Basner even made me reconsider my own relationship with my own parents."

The movie was first developed by veteran producer Alexandra Rose, working closely with two former standup-comics-turned-television writers named Rick Podell and Michael Preminger. *Nothing in Common* was their first movie script in a career that had started when they met as struggling performers in New York and casually began to rewrite one another's acts. Alexandra Rose was a native of Green Bay, Wisconsin who launched her film career in 1972 when she worked for Roger Corman's New World Pictures as assistant national sales manager. She went on to co-produce the Oscar-winning *Norma Rae* with Tamara Asseyev and *I Wanna Hold Your Hand*, the first effort of *Back to the Future*'s Robert Zemeckis for Steven Spielberg's production company.

The script for the film came to the attention of Tom Hanks and then-president of Rastar, Howard W. Koch, Jr., both of whom had been seeking a story to develop. When those three interests—Hanks, Koch, and Rose—merged under the Rastar banner, Garry Marshall and Tri-Star Pictures became involved. Marshall, veteran producer of TV series like *Happy Days*, *Laverne and Shirley*, *Mork and Mindy*, and *The Odd Couple*, was coming off his second directorial effort, the successful Matt Dillon vehicle, *The Flamingo Kid*. He saw *Nothing in Common* as a "humorous, poignant explo-

TOM HANKS • 161

ration of how much we owe our parents, a natural progression from the sixties milieu of *The Flamingo Kid*."

"That was an age of comparative innocence," said Marshall. "When notions of thrift, hard work, and a good education were challenged by the values of the get-rich-quick society.

"There's been a lot of upward mobility in the time between the stories. The family relationship in *Nothing in Common* is more complex. It's much more of a *dramatic* comedy.

"I just felt that's what moved me—mothers, fathers, sisters, brothers, sons, daughters—I was always very interested, fascinated by it. I feel that we have so many choices in life now. Parents are one of the few choices we don't have. You can't have a parent transplant. You can't go to a doctor and get a new mother and father. And that's what we're stuck with, for better or worse. And I think that makes for a certain tension in life. There is always a love that is there and sometimes a hate. It's usually a love-hate relationship. I have always found that a tremendously absorbing subject, as well as one that's neither black nor white."

Indeed, the film's major marketing problem was getting across the movie's mixed moods. This was not another wacky Tom Hanks comedy, though there were some humorous elements to it. But, as Hanks pointed out, the film mirrored the mood changes of reality . . . and that's a difficult concept to market to the average moviegoer.

On the face of it, Tom Hanks's young advertising executive, David Basner, is a character like many others he's played. In fact, Basner is a combination of *Bosom Buddies*'s Kip Wilson (also an advertising art director), *Splash*'s Allen Bauer, *Volunteer*'s Lawrence Bourne III, and *The Money Pit*'s rock'n'roll attorney Walter Fielding. When we meet him, he is a dynamic young executive on the rise, loved by his employees, respected by his bosses; a man with a witty rejoinder for every occasion and a solution to every problem. We see a young creative mind at home in his environment, and casually enjoying the fruits of his success—a lively social life featuring serial one-night stands with a variety of airline stewardesses and other uniformed ladies.

All well and good. Enter David's father, one aging childrenswear salesman named Max, played by Jackie Gleason, who announces suddenly that his wife, David's mom Lorraine (Eva Marie Saint), has walked out on him after thirty-four years of marriage. All of a sudden, the Yuppies' worst nightmare comes true— the tables have been turned on the baby boomers and their parents need *them*. It is a potent and relevant tale, and it is told with great warmth and insight in the script.

"[Podell and Preminger's] screenplay demonstrates what might be called the ideal qualities of network TV," wrote *New York* magazine's David Denby, one of the film's biggest boosters. "It's very bright, consistently entertaining, and both shrewd and decent about the ways people actually live . . . they have used the freedom that movies can give to push past commonplace expectations."

Much of the credit for that emotional resonance must go to Jackie Gleason, who gives a remarkable performance as Max Basner that's right out of *Death of a Salesman*. Ray Stark, chairman of the board of Rastar, had originally sent Gleason the script. The two had worked together on both *The Toy* and *Smokey and the Bandit.* The script arrived at Gleason's Miami home one morning and the Great One committed to the role immediately. "It was the fastest yes I ever received from a star," said Stark.

It was a dream come true for Tom Hanks, who idolized the Great One. "There was a certain amount of awe beforehand, but the first day on the set, Jackie came over to me and said, 'Howya doin' kid—let's make history.' We threw our arms around each other, embraced, and it was easy from then on."

"You're dealing with an icon when you talk about Jackie Gleason," Hanks told a syndicated radio interviewer. "And it goes beyond being the comic or the booze-hound. He's a much more complex individual than that. And when it came time to stand up in front of the camera, he didn't want to be bothered with anything that was going to take away from the concentration of the work. Jackie does not rehearse. He wants to get it right the first time. He doesn't want to take anything away from the spontaneity. He's always, 'Let's do it, c'mon,' which is a great way to work if you're acting for the movies. He's proven he can deliver the goods that way, so it works.

"I learned a lot from working with Jackie and Eva Marie Saint. Polar opposites, though, no doubt about it. What you try to do in front of a camera is very fragile. When it's not an honest gut reaction, that falsehood lands smack dab on the film stock, gets projected onto the screen, and the audience knows it. . . . "

There aren't too many of those in *Nothing in Common,* especially in the scenes between Hanks and Gleason, profiles of whom were used face-to-face in the posters displayed as advertising for the movie. The film tried to attract both Hanks's younger teenage fans and Gleason's older, middle-aged audience, and some critics pointed out that mixed mood didn't always work. The third subplot involved Hanks's wavering emotional struggle between Sela Ward's "modern naughty lady" executive, the strong-willed media director of an account he's eager to get, and theater professor Donna Mildred Martin, one of David's old flames, played by Bess Armstrong, who refused to be a rival for his affections.

Hanks did admit that he couldn't resist his beautiful *Nothing in Common* costar Sela Ward, which further exacerbated his disintegrating marriage.

"Sela is one of these women, who, on first meeting, really does take your breath away, to the point that I didn't know if I could work with a woman who was that beautiful. I felt like a jerk. And I knew that in twenty days we were going to be lying naked together. I would never have the guts to take this woman out. And yet now I'm going to play a guy who is going to hit on this babe repeatedly throughout the course of the movie."

Geez, some guys have all the luck.

During the filming of *Nothing in Common,* though, *Cosmopolitan* reported that Hanks finally separated from his wife. He moved in with an old pal from the *Bosom Buddies* days, David Chambers, not far from his San Fernando Valley home where Sam lived with their children. Chambers was an Ohio-born writer who shared a passion for the Cleveland Indians with Hanks. The two had become fast friends on the *Bosom Buddies* set and even worked on a screenplay together (*Three Guys from Cleveland*) when the TV series was yanked.

Chambers attributes his good pal's success to the fact that "he's always wide open, always confident. Even when he's highly energized, he seems relaxed, and I think that's very important, especially in film acting, where your face is forty feet high on the screen. I don't get the feeling Tom's acting so much as projecting his own personality in whatever his part is; which is, after all, the essence of film acting."

Although he doesn't think success has changed the Tom Hanks he knows, Chambers does admit, "He may have to be somewhat more defensive in public than he once was. Once your face is on TV and people recognize you, you're gonna run into people who want your autograph. He always handles that really well, at least when I've been with him."

Even while he was staying with Chambers, Hanks never let on that there was anything wrong to his colleagues on the *Nothing in Common* set. Ever the trooper, Hanks earned the praise of those involved with the film for his professionalism.

"He's one of the few young actors," said Garry Marshall, "who doesn't believe that the set should revolve around his private life."

He never has.

"He doesn't talk about his private life much," says Chambers. "When he was in the trauma of separation, he talked about it some. He opened up a little, but he needed to talk to someone. Because he couldn't handle it himself."

"I had some personal problems. Big deal.

Everybody has them," he told *Cosmopolitan*. "We're not talking about nuclear holocaust. I was a little bit crazy. What I tried to do was turn it to my advantage for my work. I really shouldn't answer questions about the woman I married. She's an actress, producer, writer, more or less. . . . In some ways, I guess I've been like a classic absentee father. My work has taken me away a lot—and certainly being separated, even more so."

And yet Hanks refused to blame the breakup on the strains of his newfound success or his acting career.

"I don't believe that. I think my marriage broke up for any of the reasons that any other marriage breaks up. Lack of communication plays a huge part, and the basic nature of the relationship."

In the *Los Angeles Times*, he took the same tack: "My work didn't ruin my marriage. You can't put the blame on the film business. It's just as hard working at a bank and staying happily married as it is doing movies."

His friend David Chambers agrees. "I don't think it was his career which broke up the marriage. I think it was more a personal thing between Tom and Sam. The dynamic of him being very successful and her being less successful would apply, though, regardless of whether it was in show business or not."

Finally, though, Tom Hanks's stardom wasn't the reason his marriage failed, nor was his lingering involvement with Rita Wilson. It was something deeper, something that Hanks's *Nothing in Common* character faced rather squarely.

"For a long time, you go through this period of swearing you'll never make the same mistakes as your parents," he told the *Los Angeles Times.* "But then you realize that they didn't really make mistakes. They just did what had to be done. That's just the way it works out sometimes."

That vulnerability comes through clearly in Hanks's scenes with Jackie Gleason. Hanks is beginning to accept his past as he's also begun to reconcile with his real father, a dialysis patient who had come close to dying, mirroring the situation in *Nothing in Common.*

"I gave Garry a hard time one day when we were getting ready to shoot this movie. I asked him, 'What if people don't care about the film?' He gave me a real pep talk. But about three months later, he came up and told me, 'You know, I lost a whole night's sleep over what you said. I kept thinking that whole night—so what if they *don't* care?' I think we really did capture something here, but you never know."

The initial critical and audience reaction was a little muted. The film came out on July 30, 1986, marking the second summer in a row that Tom Hanks had two movies out in one season. *Variety* complained, "*Nothing in Common* is the kind of film that tries to be all things to all people and as a result succeeds at none of them. Part youth comedy, part sappy family drama, pic continually seems to be tripping over itself. Only consistent element is the manic and entertaining performance of Tom Hanks as an ad exec on the way up. But even he is not likely to charm much of an audience into seeing this misdirected production."

Most publications, though, noticed the yeoman work of Hanks and Gleason, and even mentioned the latter as a candidate for a supporting actor Oscar nomination.

Time wrote, "Hanks does a masterly job of bridging the movie's moods. David is his richest, most revealing character yet . . . *Nothing in Common* hasn't fully resolved its own Oedipal struggle with Hollywood formulas, but it's in there fighting. At its best, Marshall's mixture of the bitter, the sentimental, and the jaunty is a tonic."

The *Village Voice* also praised his performance. "*Nothing in Common* is the Tom Hanks turn we've been waiting for. As a hotshot young ad exec, Hanks embodies everything we love and hate about the eighties sense of humor: its lack of conviction, its irreverence, its frank self-interest. The camera tags along as he strolls into his agency, a verbal Rambo firing japes instead of bullets; and under his steady barrage, a woman in the waiting room cracks up, a secretary blushes, colleagues fall back, charmed and speechless. . . . "

Nothing in Common marked Hanks's passage into film adulthood. The romantic illusions he'd once had were shattered by his failed marriage, but his career was, as always, stronger for it. He turned the hurt and pain in his personal life into a performance remarkable for its humor and sensitivity. The role may have served almost like therapy for him.

"My character grew up in a family that was not pleasant. This was not a happy home and he did not enjoy his parents. It was not the greatest of childhoods, but, by the time the film is over, I think he realizes that may still be the case, but they're still his parents and it's still his childhood. This was the home he grew up in. There's a bond that's deeper, more important and precious than one in which you can just dismiss it all because you want to lay blame at the feet of your parents. I think that's an important aspect of growing up. Sometimes we're lucky and understand this when we're seventeen, and other times it takes longer . . . when you're twenty-four or thirty-six or forty-five or even older. And some of us never get to that point," Hanks said in a radio interview about his *Nothing in Common* alter ego, David Basner. It's obvious he's hitting close to his own home.

"There's this one columnist who, every time I talk to her, wants to know about my hideous childhood and how I overcame it," he has said. "No matter how many times I say it wasn't that bad, it still comes across as 'look what he's lived through.' I had my older brother and sister. I'm not as close with my mom as other kids are, but it doesn't stop the fact that I love her. I say to my mom, 'I love you, but I don't know you because I didn't live with you.'"

With *Nothing in Common*, Tom Hanks made

the first tentative steps toward integrating
the part of his background he had thoroughly
repressed and sublimated into his work. That
flippant facade was gradually being chipped
away to reveal the sensitive, dreamy idealist
underneath, the "second Tom Hanks" that his
old pal Peter Scolari had already recognized.
It was one he'd explore quite thoroughly in
his first fully dramatic role since *Mazes and
Monsters*, a journey that would take him to
Israel to film Moshe Mizrahi's *Every Time We
Say Goodbye*.

11 Tom Hanks Gets Serious

"I've never done the same thing twice and how many people can say that? Some have bombed, but who cares?"

—Tom Hanks in *Esquire*

"What I do for a living is go to work and pretend I'm somebody else," Hanks told a radio interviewer. "I get to make up this whole fantasy world, of which there are very concrete laws that have to be obeyed, but they're all in my own head, nobody else has to pay attention to them. It can be a very wonderful gig. The thing about it is, not everybody can do it. That's not to pat myself on the back. I can hardly balance a checkbook nor am I able to design racing cars. Acting is what I do and, unfortunately, I can't do much of anything else. It's this or nothing. I can *pretend* to build automobiles. Actors should get diplomas because we end up picking up so much knowledge vicariously. This head of mine is filled with incredibly trivial knowledge that has slowly been accumulating because of what I've had to do and where I've had to do it."

From his itinerant upbringing to the vagabond life of a young actor, Tom Hanks has achieved a fluid, *Zelig*like ability to adapt to the situation and create a reality around it. Initially attracted to the behind-the-scenes end of a theatrical production, he has always looked on acting for the opportunities it presents to glimpse other worlds . . . and learn new skills. Each project represented such an opportunity to Hanks, and he took advantage of all of them. In *Bosom Buddies*, his pal Peter Scolari taught him how to juggle. In *Splash*, he learned how to scuba dive; in *Red Shoe*, how to play violin. In *Volunteers*, he found himself with a trip to Mexico; in *Nothing in Common*, to Chicago. For his next film, Hanks would travel to Israel to work with a one-time Academy Award-winning director in his first dramatic role in a major motion picture. Coming on the heels of six ostensible comedies in a row, it was yet another large Hanks risk to star in the movie that started out being called *Love Is Ever Young*, then *Love Hurts*, before finally being released as *Every Time We Say Goodbye*.

Typically, Hanks jumped right into the project in February, 1986, even before *The Money Pit* or *Nothing In Common* were in theaters. He didn't realize the former had opened strong and the latter had built up good word-of-mouth to the point where it grossed $23 million and drew $13.5 million in theatrical rentals, according to *Variety*. Tom was off in Israel, filming the bittersweet love story about a young American World War II pilot who falls in love, while recuperating from an injury in a Jerusalem hospital, with a beautiful, religious young Jewish girl. The movie's $3.7 million budget was the highest ever for an Israeli production, over three times what it cost director Mizrahi to direct the Oscar-winning *Madame Rosa*, another *Romeo & Juliet*-styled romance which brought together a young Arab orphan and an aging Jewish ex-prostitute/Holocaust survivor, memorably played by the late Simone Signoret in her first of two films for the Israeli filmmaker in French.

Hanks saw an opportunity, once again, to expand his horizons by working with Mizrahi.

"I was anxious to have the opportunity to work with a small group of people who do a special kind of story—out of the glare of attention," he said in the film's production notes. "Working in an intimate, nonpressured way is something new for me—we're not going off to a movie studio with parking spaces and commissaries and executives. We're just going out to make a movie where Moshe Mizrahi can concentrate on being a director instead of an executive. And I can concentrate on being an actor and not a movie star. Perhaps European actors are used to making movies this way, but I'm not. What's great about it is that there are no egos like 'This is what I want from this movie.' That's something new. And something that doesn't always happen in American movies.

"There are a number of considerations in accepting a movie role—one, of course, is getting a good part. I'm a selfish actor; I like good roles. Sometimes an actor does a movie because of its story or message. Sometimes it's the people involved. Sometimes it's the money. If you're lucky, it's everything rolled into one. And the creative challenge is much more important to me now than running around, having a good time, and making friends. The glamour of making a movie has taken a back seat to that creative aspect. From here on, it's the acting that remains to be seen."

Indeed, Hanks's choice of doing the low-profile *Every Time We Say Goodbye* makes perfect sense in the context of his own life-long commitment to his craft. Although most people saw this as his first "serious" film role, Tom was quick to dismiss that description in a *Jerusalem Post* interview that took place during the on-location shooting.

"People are going to put more weight on this film because it's a so-called drama and my other movies were so-called comedies. But I'm serious about all my roles. My job is to take a character from the typewritten pages and collaborate with the director to make him come alive.

"This movie has wit and amusing moments, but it also has sadness, and this combination of humor and warmth and sorrow is the measure of a great work that never ages or bores.

"I think that all of the great plays, in whatever language, and from whatever country, have a vast amount of wit to them. Not just laughs and comedy, but wit. Look at *Hamlet, Othello,* and *Richard III.* There's some very witty and funny stuff written into the scripts. The same thing with Chekhov in *The Cherry Orchard* and *The Three Sisters.* Even in Eugene O'Neill's supposedly down, dour plays there's wit and humor. What a bore it would be to go to a play that you know is going to be tragic and depressing and never have a light moment. There are times for tragic peaks and valleys, but you also need the energy sometimes—and it's not roaring laughter, but just laughing inside—so the audience can see the tragedy of life together with the comedy of life. And I think that is one of the important elements that makes *Every Time We Say Goodbye* special. There's great humor, great warmth, and right next to it, great sadness. I think that's the measure of a great work. That's why such works never get boring or aged. They have that element of wit that makes a classical theme come alive over and over again."

In the movie, Hanks portrays flight lieutenant David Bradford, an American who has fled to Canada in 1942 in order to join the Royal Air Force. The film opens when, after being treated in a Jerusalem hospital, he moves into a room at a boarding house where his captain and squadron leader Peter Ross has been living. Ross has met a beautiful Jewish girl whom he plans to marry, and she introduces David to her best friend, Sarah Perrara, played by the beautiful twenty-three-year-old Spanish actress Cristina Marsillach. As Sephardic Jews, Sarah and her family are descendants of a long and ancient tradition whose members share a devout and intimate religious bond exclusive to themselves. This, understandably, places a severe roadblock on the young girl's romance with David, a non-Jew and an American. The family views with horror the thought that Sarah might even contemplate a relationship with a young man who so contradicts their time-honored ways.

The idea for the movie was brought to producers Sharon Harel and Jacob Kotzky in 1984 by director Moshe Mizrahi.

"At first Moshe only had the germ of an idea," said Harel. "He told us this beautiful and simple story. We were so moved that we told him to go back and write a script for us. The result was so lovely and so touching that we had no problem finding the backing to make it. Love stories are universal."

Hanks was attracted to the classical nature of the impossible affair, and the inherent "wit" in some of the situations where worlds collide.

"It's the story of the bonding of two people, not two cultures. David comes from a wide-open American society where it's not unusual to rebel against your family. I see him as a loner who wandered around the U.S. for a while during the great Depression, when a mass of humanity wandered around without a lot to do.

"In this film you see people from such divergent social backgrounds that don't understand each other totally, and yet communicate with incredible, deep feeling. When David goes to Sarah's house and tries to understand what's going on around him, it's very funny. Really funny. Some people may think it's low comedy, but it's not at all. It's the funny way that life can be. It's like when you are walking down the street and you see something so funny that it makes you laugh for days, and then right next to it there can be something so sad that it makes you cry."

When Sharon Harel was asked if the cultural push-pull between Sarah and David might stand for the greater political tension that surrounds present-day Israel, she laughed off any such hyperbole. "People think that filming in Israel is dangerous. It simply isn't true. We have the best security in the world in this country. There was only one instance where we had to delay shooting—there had been a bomb scare at a market in Jericho. But even that was a false alarm. I assure you it really and truly is safe. If we could only convince people of that. . . . You want to know what the most frightening thing is about filming in Israel? The *insurance rates*!!"

Tom Hanks, in turn, echoed the Israeli producer's amusement at the presumed danger in the Middle East. "I wouldn't want to rush through a place like Jerusalem. It's a city that you want to roam. And in Tel Aviv, I wanted to see how people decorate their apartments, what their political views are, and since there weren't as many camels as I expected, what kind of cars they drive. You don't have to be religious to understand the worldwide importance of Israel. This is essentially where all western societies find their base. And the history here is the greatest story every told. As an American, and a gentile, I envy the rich Jewish heritage. But what really interests me is how people live today. How they relate to one another, and what they do on a Saturday night."

That same curiosity and observational powers have made Hanks such a fine actor.

Every Time We Say Goodbye allowed Tom to spend time away from the pressure-cooker atmosphere of Hollywood and his burgeoning stardom, which was becoming more and more of a burden to him.

"It's terrible what they've done to Sean Penn and people like him," he told *Cosmopolitan*. "They can't walk down the street, they can't go out to dinner. The press, the guys who write the gossip. I hate the way they attack. They do it to him, they'll do it to somebody else, then they'll do it to me. Just look at how it affects a young actor's work. Look what happened to Sean Penn in his last movie. Look at Tom Cruise, the way he walks, the way he talks. He's losing it as an actor. He's becoming a movie star. He's on the wrong track."

"The sunglasses, the autographs, and limousines are just gossamer," he told the *Jerusalem Post*. "What really counts are the periods of very intense concentration on the film set, when your emotions run at a fever pitch. A movie set is a very exciting place to be, filled with dedicated people doing jobs they're very good at. You have to learn discipline and concentration real fast, or you're going to get eaten alive."

As for the perks of his job, Hanks can do fine without them, thank you.

"You have all these secretaries. Limos pick you up at the airport and people bring you diet caffeine-free Cokes all the time and tell you you're fabulous, the show you're working on is great—until it comes out," he said sarcastically. "And then you're yesterday's Danish."

Which is just what happened when *Every Time We Say Goodbye* finally premiered in New York on November 14, 1986. The *New York Times* reported, "Tom Hanks is utterly out of place in this Israeli romance for at least two reasons: because there's something so innately comic about him, even in solemn surroundings, and because he has so much more energy than the film does . . . this love story is mostly notable for its strained, awkward small talk and its long, long pauses."

It is a case of Tom Hanks's vivid comic persona getting in the way of his attempt at a dramatic portrayal. (It also harks back to Peter Scolari's remark that the one side of

Hanks's personality would mock the other, more serious side.) The *Times*'s film critic apparently felt the same way, just waiting during those pregnant moments for Hanks to crack a joke. Not that the film was all solemn, as both Hanks and a *Variety* reviewer noted. The show biz bible insisted that the film's draw "will be watching an effective Hanks in this warm, though slow-paced, film . . . the movie is not devoid of humor. Early scenes when Hanks is accepted to dinner by the family as a friend and not yet a suitor are funny and believable. Culturally rich story is aided throughout by the pic's all-Israel shoot, nicely highlighting the different worlds these two lovers come from."

Unfortunately, that wasn't enough for most filmgoers. The movie had a limited release to start with—it never did open in Los Angeles—and quickly and quietly disappeared from New York theaters within a couple of weeks. For Tom Hanks, it was an experiment that might have failed at the box office, but certainly didn't sidetrack his still-hot momentum. In fact, over the next six months, Hanks would be more in demand than ever, with a heightened media profile and three roles in major motion pictures—*Dragnet,*

Punchline, and *Big.* There would be no time to sit back and contemplate failure for this young star.

"I'm still real interested in what I do, that's why I work so much. I didn't get into this to have any sort of power, to dress in sharkskin suits or something like that . . . I enjoy what I do, and sometimes I do real well and sometimes I stink. And when I stink, I feel real bad, but when I do good, I feel good. Just because a person isn't 'successful' doesn't mean everything is hunky-dory in the rest of their lives."

Indeed, Tom's separation from Samantha was turning into messy divorce proceedings, while his relationship with actress Rita Wilson was heating up on the back burner.

12 Into the Future: *Dragnet, Punchline, Big and Beyond*

"[I started acting out of] a desire to have fun. . . . It's not so much that [acting] was hugely challenging or broadened my horizons—which were both true—but simply because it was fun. That's why I got into this in the first place. And fun comes out of challenge and out of struggle. If you don't have that, how can you enjoy the other side of it?"
—Tom Hanks

By the time he finished filming both *Nothing in Common* and *Every Time We Say Goodbye*, it was the spring of 1986 and Tom Hanks must have been feeling pretty drained.

"Those two films required a lot of not just concentration, but also emotional investment, which is very, very exhausting," Hanks said. "I don't think it's particularly good for your psyche, because you find yourself analyzing so many things. Eventually, you can drive yourself crazy."

As a bit of a hiatus, then, Hanks took his first-ever supporting role opposite yet another former Second City comic, Dan Aykroyd, in a parody remake of the classic TV detective series, *Dragnet*. In the role originally planned for old buddy John Candy, Hank plays Pep Streebeck, a modern cop forced to ride with a partner—Dan Aykroyd's Joe Friday—who is emotionally locked in the 1950s.

"I just took the job as a hired gun, and it makes me nervous," Hanks admitted. "Dan has this Joe Friday that he's doing that is set in stone. Next to that, if I so much as raise an eyebrow it's like screaming at the top of my lungs. Dan is Joe Friday all the time; he's got that kind of analytical mind. It's very much Dan's movie, so much so that I wonder where I fit in."

The big-budget Universal movie is being helmed by first-time director Tom Mankiewicz, known previously as screenwriter for the James Bond thrillers *Live and Let Die* and *Diamonds Are Forever* as well as *Superman I* and *II* and the medieval epic, *Ladyhawke*.

Aykroyd plays the deadpan namesake nephew of Detective Sergeant Joe Friday, the role originally made famous by the late, poker-faced Jack Webb. Harry Morgan is even on hand to recreate the part of Bill Gannon.

"I wear a gun, I flash a badge, I punch some guys out, I jump in the car with Dan, and off we go," Hanks remarked about the film, which seemed to satisfy his criteria for a movie that would let him have some fun.

Aykroyd has also admitted to a long-time fascination with the character of Joe Friday. "Next to Clouseau, he's the most famous cop in the world," he said. "I've studied his speech inflections, his mannerisms, his walk. During filming, I'd listen to tapes of the old shows. I even started dreaming in character. If there ever was a character I'd always wanted to play, it was this one."

Hanks came aboard as the straitlaced sarge's hip, streetwise partner Pep Streebeck.

"I read the script and found myself laughing out loud," he stated. "I loved the idea of working with Dan and I liked the character. He's loose, quick, a little unconventional— the perfect balance to Friday."

Costarring with Aykroyd and Hanks are veteran screen actors Christopher Plummer as the ambitious Reverend Whirley and Dabney Coleman as porn king Jerry Caesar. Beautiful Alexandra Paul is the chaste, charming Connie Swail, who falls hard for Friday. Rounding out the cast are Harry Morgan as Gannon, Joe Friday's loyal partner from the television show, whose years of service have now earned him the rank of captain. Elizabeth Ashley is the austere police commissioner Jane Kirkpatrick and Jack O'Halloran is the sinister saboteur Emil Muzz.

"Our film is a comedic homage to one of the truly classic television shows," said director Mankiewicz. "With utmost reverence toward our source material, we've created new characters and a plot of much grander scale than anything the TV show could ever have attempted."

Joe Friday was first introduced as a character on the NBC radio program, *Dragnet*, in 1949. As conceived by Webb himself, the show was based on real police cases and procedures. The entertainment world's most recognizable four-note theme ("Dum-de-dum-dum") announced the series's TV debut on January 3, 1952. It ran for seven-and-a-half years, then left the air to return in January, 1967, before stamping its final "Badge 714" trademark in September, 1970. Two feature-length dramatic films based on the series were produced, one released theatrically in 1954, the other made for TV in 1969. The show also inspired a pair of hit 1953 records in Ray

Anthony's recording of the Walter Schumann theme and Stan Freeberg's comedic takeoff, "St. George and the Dragnet," which sold over one million copies.

"*Dragnet* set the tone for all the realistic police shows that followed," explained Aykroyd. "All those shows took their inspiration from that famous opening: 'This is the city. Los Angeles, California. Four thousand square miles of modern humanity.' That introduction established an attitude that helped reshape television programming.

"I believe good comedy should have a base in realism. I think that's part of why the *Dragnet* series lends itself so well to comedy. It had a very recognizable style. We've got more going on here than simply me doing Joe Friday. Alan Zweibel [who cowrote the screenplay with Aykroyd], Mankiewicz, and I are using Jack Webb's writing style and the deliberate pacing of the show. I'm a tremendous Jack Webb fan. I loved everything he did.

"*Dragnet* was something I'd always wanted to do but I never thought the opportunity would come up because I didn't know who owned the rights to the idea. When Universal called and said they were interested in doing it, I think I made a deal to write the script the next week."

Producer David Permut, who first approached MCA with an idea to make a comedy based on the *Dragnet* characters, thought that Aykroyd as Friday was perfect.

"This very stylized dramatic show suddenly seemed like the kind of thing that would ideally lend itself to comedy."

He interested both Aykroyd and executive producer Bernie Brillstein, then enlisted former *Saturday Night Live* writer Zweibel to work with Dan and Tom Mankiewicz on a screenplay. The original choice for Friday's partner, John Candy, had previous commitments that made him unavailable, so the producers turned to Hanks.

"The chemistry between Friday and his partner is what made *Dragnet* work the first time," said Permut. "The chemistry between Aykroyd and Hanks is what makes this picture work."

"I've always been lucky in being matched up with first-rate actors throughout my career," Hanks has stated. "Dan and I met each other and instantly knew we were going to have a blast making this movie. It was great working again with someone from Second City. I'd worked with both Jim Belushi and John Candy, so I've always felt real comfortable around folks from that group.

"In this movie, audiences will be seeing two of the world's most famous fictional cops, Joe Friday and his partner . . . who was his partner anyway?

"You've gotta have some kinda spin going in. Sometimes there's a little more written out about the guy but in this case there wasn't. So, between talking with Dan and making up a bunch of stuff myself, we managed to put this guy together.

"I always figured he was in the air force or something and came really close to being thrown out. Now he's in the police department and he's really close to being thrown out. He's someone who likes being a cop but he's easily bored by what he perceives as the trivialities of the job: filling out forms, following proper procedure. The sort of things that Friday thrives on."

The film's producers are banking on the contrasting styles of Aykroyd as Friday and Hanks as Streebeck to be the major source of comedy in *Dragnet*. While Aykroyd is playing Friday pretty close to the vest, Hanks's Streebeck is a drastic change from Webb's TV partners.

"He's a great guy, a good cop," explained Hanks. "He likes police work when it's like a TV show, you know, with guns blazing and tires squealing. He's just not a Joe Friday kind of cop. Friday is Americana. It was very appropriate that when Jack Webb passed away they gave him a full-page obituary in *Rolling Stone* because, really, for two generations of Americans, he was the embodiment of fair play and honesty and playing by the rules. The incorruptible cop.

"You won't get the long speech from Pep that you'd get from Joe Friday, but you'll still get the bad guy dragged off in the end. Of course, on the way to the station, he might get dangled over a freeway overpass just to rattle his cage a little. But Pep's a loyal partner. He lives by the unwritten law that you do anything for your partner because . . . well, because he's your partner."

Producer Robert K. Weiss is also one who has noted the uniqueness of the character portrayed by Tom Hanks. "He's a pretty wild individual. He's been transferred out of vice for practicing somewhat exotic police techniques. He also has a major problem with authority and rebels against the establishment. So, we take him and put him with a straight-arrow like Friday and that's where we have some fun. These two try to get along and during the course of the investigation they not only become buddies but actually start to take on some of each other's characteristics."

The movie concerns Friday and Streebeck's attempt to rescue a ballet-slippered Cinderella named Connie Swail, played by Alexandra Paul, who has slipped into the clutches of a maniacal band of hedonistic zealots who call themselves P.A.G.A.N. (People Against Goodness and Normalcy). Our heroes suspect this terrorist organization to be behind a massive conspiracy that threatens Los Angeles, but they have a tough time proving it.

The movie was shot almost entirely on and around the streets of Los Angeles, with locations including a sunny Venice beach and a seedy section of downtown. Cameras rolled in front of the gates to the exclusive Bel Aire residential section, then segued to a *barrio* in the northern part of the San Fernando Valley. Scenes were filmed inside Pasadena's newly renovated Brown Derby restaurant and outside in below-freezing winds in the Mojave Desert. One of the more unusual sites was the Angel's Gate Cultural Center in San Pedro, a World War II munitions bunker that was partially excavated and restored for the film.

"We've done our research and taken great pain to recreate and revitalize the form that Jack Webb created for TV," concluded Aykroyd in the film's production kit. "The essence of the film is consistent with what he believed in, the speeches are speeches he could have written himself, and the delivery is the way he would have done it.

"It's all in the spirit of affection for a piece of American pop culture that my generation grew up on that's also had a significant impact on kids of today. I hope people who recognize the old show will get a laugh from the recognition. And I think those who are too young to remember will quickly discover the humor and pathos in these characters and, hopefully, leave the theater wanting to see some of those old programs. Then maybe they'll come back and find a whole other level of things to laugh about."

Tom Hanks added his own benediction.

"Just smile down on us, Jack, 'cause it's in the spirit of love and good fun. We're giving them the facts, Jack. Just the facts."

The advance word on the movie, which was scheduled to open in June 1987, was guarded optimism. The publicity mills were already churning by early spring, with a Tom Hanks cover story and fashion spread in *Esquire* and a photo layout on *Dragnet* in *Life*'s special 100th birthday salute to Hollywood. From these pics, it would appear that Tom Hanks's Pep favors a yo-yo as his main prop.

Despite the failure of *Every Time We Say Goodbye*, Hanks's star was still in the ascendant, but it was during this period that his divorce from Samantha became official. He was still understandably bitter about the demands placed on him by the media; he still wanted to remain the regular guy, even though that was becoming increasingly impossible. He told one reporter who saw him turn down an autograph request, "I don't usually do this because, if I give it to one person, I have to give it to everybody, and everything is ruined—my time with my kids, my time with my girlfriend, my privacy. Everything about my life becomes Hollywood.

"I like being able to go to baseball games and sit in the stands, not in some private box with the owner of the team. I don't even request tickets for Disneyland. I stood in line at the Egyptian Theater last Friday night. It was great. Now, I can't do that if I drive up in a stretch limousine.

"I've caused pandemonium in drugstores and things like that. I'm going to get a sandwich and the person won't make the sandwich because she won't believe that I'm standing there asking her for a sandwich. And she can't talk. And I say, 'Look, just relax, yes, yes, yes, it's me.' The trappings of all this stuff are very nice, and it makes your life easier, but it's not the stuff that makes it fun. The *work* makes it fun."

Once again, he pointed out that acting is no big deal, just a job like any other.

"I've always been amazed at guys who can lay bricks or build something or play the piano," he said. "The reason why they do it so well is because, at one point, it was fun. As they grow older and more proficient, they end up challenging themselves in order to do it better, and, when you see something like that, you say, 'Hey, I did a good job and it was fun.' That's the way I feel more often than not when it's all over with and the product is out there. That's the highest praise."

Working on *Dragnet* offered him an opportunity to sit back and polish his craft without worrying about carrying the picture, he has admitted.

"I used to feel I could just bully myself through something and drive on pure adrenaline. I can see that it's pointless. And it's a very good lesson to learn as a professional actor as well as a human being."

Despite all his protestations, though, Tom Hanks is more than your Average Joe. The clothes he's seen wearing in his *Esquire* spread, for instance, include a $130 vest, a $47.50 shirt, a $250 pair of linen trousers, $215 Spectator shoes, $21 socks, and a $32 belt, for a grand total of $695.50. You can't dress like that on an Average Joe's salary, that's for sure.

Right after finishing filming *Dragnet,* Hanks plunged into yet another movie, this one as part of his Columbia development deal. It is a film about a pair of aspiring standup comedians, to star Tom and Sally Field. The movie began shooting in March, 1987, with writer-director David Seltzer, who had previously received praise for the gentle high school comedy, *Lucas*. It was being produced by Field's own Fogwood Productions for distribution by Columbia Pictures.

As part of the preproduction preparation, both Hanks and Field were coached by what Seltzer called his Comic Bodyguards, a group of top comics who taught the pair delivery and timing before sending them out to hone their acts in front of live comedy audiences in New York and Los Angeles nightclubs.

Field plays a housewife/would-be comedienne who meets a "neurotic, unstable but brilliant comic" (Hanks) and the two try to help each other "down the road to Oz."

Seltzer auditioned more than 150 professional comics for supporting parts, discovering so much talent—both male and female—"that I'm casting some in roles that have nothing to do with comedy," he told the *Los Angeles Times*.

Hanks himself had to eat the words he once delivered to producer Brian Grazer when he auditioned for *Splash* and told him he would never do standup comedy because he was "chickenshit" at it. For his part in *Punchline*, Hanks made surprise appearances at both Igby's and the Comedy Store in Los Angeles, in front of audiences that included Gallagher, Howie Mandel, and Jimmy Walker. In New York, he interned at the Comic Strip on Second Avenue on the Upper East Side, where he did two nights of live appearances for twenty-five minutes each night.

At the club, Hanks's material included pokes at Iranians, superheroes, and Sylvester Stallone. He told jokes about doctors ("They look at our wives' breasts; why can't we look at *theirs*?") and junkies ("The doc gives you drugs which he hopes will make you feel better; the dealer gives you drugs which he *knows* will make you feel better."). One routine, as reported by New York's *Daily News* columnist Cindy Adams, was on not being an angry young man, although "the clown at the bank says it takes twelve days to clear a check." Hanks also said subways were originally submarine tunnels, but it took twelve hours to get anywhere so they pumped out the water and put in tracks. He finished by portraying a Jewish waiter staggering under a heavy tray, complaining, "We carry the weight of Israel on our shoulders."

Adams quoted the Comic Strip's talent coordinator, Lucien Hold, as saying Hanks showed a lot of promise. "Tom was good. The audience loved him. The more he did, the better he was."

The film is scheduled for release in the fall of 1987.

With *Dragnet* due out in June, Hanks's public profile began to pick up. He was one of the presenters at the Academy Awards ceremony in March 1987, and boldly arrived with girlfriend Rita Wilson on his arm. Hanks presented the award for best animated short film accompanied by an animated Bugs Bunny in one of the program's highlights. Unfortunately, Tom had a great opportunity to ad-lib something about being upstaged by a rabbit, but he didn't take the bait. Like the professional he is, he let Bugs steal the show . . . which was cool.

No sooner did he finish filming *Punchline*, then he was on to yet another major project. This time, he was inked for the film, *Big*, about a young child transferred in a grown-up's body after playing a game at a carnival, directed by Penny Marshall and produced by Jim Brooks for 20th Century Fox. Hanks was tapped after the role was turned down by Warren Beatty, who wanted $7.5 million to star, and then Robert DeNiro, who was announced for the film but bowed out when his $3 million upfront asking price was nixed. Once again, it looked like Tom Hanks would end up smelling like a rose. As the summer of 1987 came around, Tom Hanks still hadn't stopped working.

"I'm not the kind of guy who can spend a lot of time by myself, in all honesty," he told a magazine interviewer. "A friend of mine told me to take up golf, but I can't because it's too stupid a game. The only game show I can watch is *Jeopardy*, because it goes so fast. You have eight thousand questions coming at you faster than you can even answer. *That's* my speed."

13 What Is Tom Hanks Really Like? A Critical Assessment

"Cary Grant never got starstruck on himself; he never seemed to be saying, Look at me. The most obvious characteristic of his acting is the absence of narcissism—the outgoingness to the audience."

—Pauline Kael

What makes Tom Hanks a top movie star, capable of commanding a per-picture salary of around $1 million? After all, he's only had two out-and-out box office smashes with *Splash* and *Bachelor Party*, and scattered good reviews for *Volunteers* and *Nothing in Common*. What is it that makes the thirty-one-year-old actor one of America's favorite stars? Within a few months in 1987, he was nominated by the Nickelodeon children's network as one of the younger folks' most popular performers, and was also honored by the Academy of Comic Arts for his role in *Nothing in Common*. He's been compared throughout his career to legends like Jack Lemmon, Cary Grant, Jimmy Stewart, but he'll have none of it, even though those actors are his idols.

"They said I was Jimmy Stewart. They said I was Jack Lemmon. Now they say I'm Cary Grant. Next they'll say I'm John Wayne," he has said derisively. "So much of what you do has been influenced by what those guys did. They were on the cutting edge, inventing screen acting along with the creation of the thing itself. Every time one of them goes, an era is over."

As for the immortal Archie Leach, who had just passed away, Hanks dismissed any comparisons as "an insult to Mr. Grant . . . but if you're going to be compared with anyone, it might as well be Cary Grant. Who wouldn't want to be Cary Grant?"

About the other actors he's most often mentioned in the same breath with, Hanks had kind words for both Jack Lemmon and Jimmy Stewart.

"Lemmon could take a picture like *The Apartment*, which is so funny yet at the same time so sad, so bittersweet, and then sandwich it right next to *The Days of Wine and Roses*. What you get from him is an incredible joy at being an actor and working in movies that really jumps at you from the screen."

He is equally as enthusiastic about Jimmy Stewart. "As a kid, I was always impressed with him. He had a funny voice and was kind of geeky-looking—not ugly, like a mug staring you in the face—but kind of geeky-looking. Yet he was still the hero, an Everyman hero. That's me. I'm no great-looking guy. I can get out of the ballpark if the clothes fit, but basically I have this body to work with, and I get on with it."

Which is kinda where we came in. What *is* the appeal of this funny-looking guy with the doughboy nose and woolly hair? How did he get *so* popular?

"I don't have the slightest idea why I'm successful," he has insisted. "If I did, I'd write a book: *Tom Hanks's Nine Tips for Success.* Nobody knows whether a film will do well. The success of any movie is a real crapshoot."

Ironically, Tom Hanks has succeeded in spite of his films' failures, and that brings up at least two important reasons for his fame: home video and cable. Those two media have made

Tom Hanks a familiar household commodity. While not too many people actually saw *Volunteers*, *The Man with One Red Shoe*, and *The Money Pit* in the theaters, quite a lot of people saw them on videocassette and/or cable. Likewise with *Bosom Buddies*—those who didn't catch up with the short-lived series when it debuted back in 1980 have caught episodes on syndication, where they are probably more widely viewed than they were the first time around. Tom Hanks is a 1980s movie star who has always translated well to the small screen. He is user-friendly, affable, and accessible. You want to invite him into your house to get to know him better.

The question as to what the off-screen, private Tom Hanks is really like is one that's a little more difficult to answer. The *Los Angeles Times* has said he's the kind of guy who drives a gray VJ Jetta, hasn't read *Less Than Zero*, and prefers an authentic 1950s L.A. coffeeshop like Ships to the pseudo Johnny Rocket's. He's also the kind of guy who, when he took violin lessons for *Red Shoe*, learned how to play both Rimsky-Korsakov's *Scheherazade* and the theme from *Father Knows Best*.

For many of his friends, he is exactly as

we see him on screen: warm, witty, quick with a quip, the cuddly guy-next-door who's got the answer to every question. For others, who know him better, there is a very serious side to Tom Hanks, a questioning part of his personality that drives him to succeed in the highly competitive world of film acting. It is a side that Tom doesn't let too many people view.

"Everybody had the feeling they knew him well," said Moshe Mizrahi about the filming of *Every Time We Say Goodbye*. "And yet no one knew him really."

And that's the key to understanding Tom Hanks. Underneath all the hipness and cool is a religious, spiritual individual who may feel a little guilty about his fame and fortune, but who nevertheless worked hard to achieve it and isn't about to give it up. Why should he?

One of Hanks's favorite Hollywood tales illustrates well his own self-effacing philosophy. It seems Henry Fonda had just finished a movie and was on a plane to New York along with Jimmy Stewart. They started talking and asked each other how things were going. Fonda said, "Oh, I don't know. Every time I finish one of these movies, I think people are going to catch on to the fact that I don't have the slightest idea of what I'm doing and I'll never get another job." And Stewart merely replied, "You think that, too?"

Tom Hanks doesn't have all that much to worry about in that regard. It is his very human vulnerability, something he has in common with Everyman, which has made him one of Hollywood's leading lights. Sure, he's scared, just like you and just like me, but he's channeled that fright into a gallery of regular guys who rise above their normalcy because they dare to dream . . . *and* fall on their faces.

FILMOGRAPHY

HE KNOWS YOU'RE ALONE
(1980/MGM-UA)

Costars: Don Scardino
              Caitlin O'Heaney
Director: Armand Mastroianni

RONA JAFFE'S MAZES AND MONSTERS
(1981/Made for TV)

Costars: Chris Makepeace
              Wendy Crewson
Director: Steven H. Stern
Video: Karl-Lorimar

SPLASH
(1984/Touchstone)

Costars: Daryl Hannah
              John Candy
Director: Ron Howard
Video: Touchstone

BACHELOR PARTY
(1984/Fox)

Costars: Adrian Zmed
              Tawny Kitaen
Director: Neal Israel
Video: CBS/Fox

THE MAN WITH ONE RED SHOE
(1985/Fox)

Costars:	Lori Singer
	Jim Belushi
Director:	Stan Dragoti
Video:	CBS/Fox

VOLUNTEERS
(1985/Tri-Star)

Costars:	John Candy
	Rita Wilson
Director:	Nicholas Meyer
Video:	Thorn/EMI

THE MONEY PIT
(1986/Universal)

Costars:	Shelley Long
	Alexander Godunov
Director:	Richard Benjamin
Video:	MCA Home Video

NOTHING IN COMMON
(1986/Tri-Star)

Costars:	Jackie Gleason
	Eva Marie Saint
Director:	Garry Marshall
Video:	HBO/Cannon

EVERY TIME WE SAY GOODBYE
(1986/Tri-Star)

Costars:	Cristina Marsillach
	Benedict Taylor
Director:	Moshe Mizrahi

DRAGNET
(1987/Universal)

Costars:	Dan Aykroyd
	Alexandra Paul
Director:	Tom Mankiewicz

PUNCHLINE
(1987/Columbia)

Costar:	Sally Field
Director:	David Seltzer

BIG
(1988/Fox)

Director:	Penny Marshall

Also: *Bosom Buddies* TV series for two seasons (1980–82) with Peter Scolari for Paramount Television; additional guest shots on *Family Ties* (1981), *Happy Days* (1980), and *Taxi* (1980).

ABOUT THE AUTHOR

Roy Trakin is a pop culture journalist whose work has appeared in *Musician*, *Creem*, *Melody Maker*, *Mix*, and *USA Today*. He is currently editor of the monthly publication *Playback* and features editor at *Hits* magazine. He has previously written *Sting and the Police* and served as associate editor on *Strawberry Fields Forever*, both for Ballantine Books. A Brooklyn native, he's followed the Dodgers to Los Angeles, where he lives on an acre of land with his wife, Jill Merrill.

THE BRIGHTEST STARS...

MERYL STREEP: RELUCTANT SUPERSTAR by Diana Maychick
The first biography of this dazzling, articulate film star. With 8 pages
of photos.
_____ 90246-8 $3.50 U.S.   _____ 90248-4 $4.50 Can.

ROBERT DE NIRO: THE HERO BEHIND THE MASKS by Keith McKay
A revealing look at one of today's most brilliant actors. Includes 16
pages of photos.
_____ 90475-4 $3.95 U.S.   _____ 90476-2 $4.95 Can.

ROBERT DUVALL: HOLLYWOOD MAVERICK by Judith Slawson
Leading the new breed of Hollywood hero. With 8 pages of dramatic
photos.
_____ 90422-3 $3.95 U.S.   _____ 90423-1 $4.95 Can.

KATHLEEN TURNER by Rebecca Stefoff
The first biography of Hollywood's newest, sexy—and very daring—
superstar. With 8 pages of glorious photos.
_____ 90604-8 $3.50 U.S.   _____ 90605-6 $4.50 Can.

ST. MARTIN'S PRESS—MAIL SALES
175 Fifth Avenue, New York, NY 10010

Please send me the book(s) I have checked above. I am enclosing a check or
money order (not cash) for $_____ plus 75¢ per order to cover postage and
handling (New York residents add applicable sales tax).

Name _____

Address_____

City _____ State_____ Zip Code_____
       Allow at least 4 to 6 weeks for delivery   30